Vintage Knowledge for 21st-Century Principals

Vintage Knowledge for 21st-Century Principals

A Continuum of Approaches and Success Strategies

2nd Edition

Barbara D. Culp

ROWMAN & LITTLEFIELD
Lanham • Boulder • New York • London

Published by Rowman & Littlefield
An imprint of The Rowman & Littlefield Publishing Group, Inc.
4501 Forbes Boulevard, Suite 200, Lanham, Maryland 20706
www.rowman.com

86-90 Paul Street, London EC2A 4NE, United Kingdom

Copyright © 2023 by Barbara D. Culp

All rights reserved. No part of this book may be reproduced in any form or by any electronic or mechanical means, including information storage and retrieval systems, without written permission from the publisher, except by a reviewer who may quote passages in a review.

British Library Cataloguing in Publication Information Available

Library of Congress Cataloging-in-Publication Data

Names: Culp, Barbara D., 1947– author.
Title: Vintage knowledge for 21st-century principals : a continuum of approaches and success strategies / Barbara D. Culp.
Other titles: Vintage knowledge for principals | Vintage knowledge for twenty-first century principals
Description: 2nd edition. | Lanham, Maryland : Rowman & Littlefield, [2023] | First edition: 2016. | Includes bibliographical references. | Summary: "This book will be a good tool in planning and implementing plans for school improvement and continued student growth"— Provided by publisher.
Identifiers: LCCN 2023005048 (print) | LCCN 2023005049 (ebook) | ISBN 9781475871197 (cloth) | ISBN 9781475871203 (paperback: | ISBN 9781475871210 (epub)
Subjects: LCSH: School principals—United States. | Educational leadership—United States. | School management and organization—United States.
Classification: LCC LB2831.92 .C85 2023 (print) | LCC LB2831.92 (ebook) | DDC 371.2/012—dc23/eng/20230221
LC record available at https://lccn.loc.gov/2023005048
LC ebook record available at https://lccn.loc.gov/2023005049

To my beloved husband, Oscar, our two adult children, Melisa and Dwayne, I thank you for tolerating my constant desire to write over the years. To my grandchildren and great grandchildren, I hope you find your niche in life and pursue it with passion. To the countless family, friends, and colleagues who were there to inspire me; thank you!

*Heights by great men reached and kept
Were not attained by sudden flight;
But they, while their companions slept,
Were toiling upward in the night.*

—Henry Wadsworth Longfellow

Contents

Foreword	xi
Preface	xiii
Acknowledgments	xv
Introduction	xvii
Chapter 1: Wisdom for Your School	1
Chapter 2: Wisdom for Your People	43
Chapter 3: Wisdom for You	81
Final Words: Always a Principal	121
About the Author	123

Foreword

"Improve public education." We educators (and citizens) hear this lament often. Its clarion call echoes through legislative halls and public meetings, PTA meetings, and Board of Education Meetings.

Solutions come from everyone. Everyone who attended public or private school is certain that if only educators would adopt their panacea, test scores would rise and the plethora of problems which exist in today's schools would disappear. Sadly, very few of the solutions tried in the last two decades have had any effect upon student learning.

Nor does the public believe that educators are incapable of solving educational and social problems. Frequently they are expected to do more with less resources. Smaller budgets, fewer teaching days, larger class sizes, fewer supplies, and less nonclassroom staff have been the rule. Even net pay for educators has been reduced by (unpaid) furlough days and higher insurance premiums.

In this book, Dr. Culp makes clear her belief that there are no magic solutions to resolving the problems that leaders face in public education. Leadership can be a lonely role; principals need the faith in their own abilities and the strength of their convictions if goals of school improvement and student growth are to be attained.

Dr. Culp has provided a framework for identifying many of the problems that today's principals face, and with clarity, has suggested how each can be used as a basis for analysis and planning. She is a believer in careful collection and analysis of data, cooperative planning with parents and teachers, implementation of those plans, followed by continued evaluation of the results achieved.

Principals will find themselves returning frequently to this book for continued inspiration and clarification of the path ahead. The book does not contain answers, but rather highlights areas for exploration and improvement.

In closing, I assure you that I observed Dr. Culp as the able leader of a large, elementary school which was known for its innovation and instructional improvement. I commend her book to you as a useful tool for principals and other school leaders. I also commend her book to you as a tool in planning and implementing plans for school improvement and continued student growth.

—Joan K. Zion
Retired Assistant Superintendent of Elementary Education
Atlanta Public Schools
Atlanta, Georgia

Preface

In these pages, you will find a number of ideas that supported me and allowed me to enjoy forty-plus exceptional years doing what I loved. My hope is that at least a few words of wisdom will spark something in your own heart. Perhaps one of the entries will seem practical enough for you to implement. Another might strike a chord with you personally and will guide your efforts at your school.

No matter how many words of wisdom touch you or the nature of your response, I encourage you to flip through this collection when times are tough . . . and when times are good! A second or third encounter with a specific bit of wisdom might spark new thoughts or a different perspective. Every day at your school you will grow, change, and adapt. My hope is that every time you return to this collection, my words and thoughts will help you continue to grow, change, and adapt.

Your job is one of the toughest in the world. Certainly, there are more dangerous jobs and ones that are more physically demanding. But nothing, in my opinion, requires more sweat or a larger heart than being a principal. State and federal rules will change, and teaching methods will come and go. Students will grow older, graduate, and move on to lives built on the foundation you provided. Parents will move away from your community, new families will arrive, and your staff will change. The one constant is you.

You are the leader and head cheerleader. You are the chief creative officer and the shepherd. At times you'll serve as a counselor for students and parents; at other times, you'll be the focal point for their disappointment. You're the point person for the educational organization known as a school. You're the scout who seeks the best path forward.

You are the guardian of your campus's safety and the safety of young personalities. You are all these things wrapped up in one!

Own it. Be it. Cultivate your own wisdom, and everyone at your school will benefit.

Acknowledgments

This book is dedicated to the school principals who date all the way back to the 1700s. Their experience in the classroom elevated them as the "principal" teachers of one-, two-, and three-room schoolhouses. These principal teachers took on the intensive administrative work of running a school while continuing to teach. In many instances, they received no additional pay but were expected to do the Christian thing. Their positions lifted their status in the community.

The role eventually led to the creation of the official position of school principal. The job was not easy, but it was necessary. These pioneers faced very long days without guidelines. They forged ahead doing whatever was necessary. Many left home early every morning and walked a frozen road before starting the fire that would warm the schoolhouse. They chopped the wood and fetched the water. They begged and borrowed books, and patched the ones they had to make them last.

At times, some principals spent the night at school during the worst weather to safeguard the building. Others took students and staff to school in their own vehicles. Many purchased the food and cooked the meals, purchased supplies, and in some instances served as the janitor. In some regions, the only pay they received was fresh fruits, vegetables, a pie, or some cured meat. A few got a place to stay . . . with stipulations.

All went far above and beyond the call of duty to make their schools comfortable, safe, and a good place for teaching and learning. They did it because it was the right thing to do.

They did it because they took pride as a school leader who made sure students could learn.

Today, we stand on the shoulders of those who led without formal training and with little or no pay. We owe a debt to the principals who achieved excellence against tremendous odds. With our training and official appointments, we can live up to our calling. We can continue the work they began and provide a quality education to every child.

Introduction

During a recent school visit, the principal heard that I had been a principal for much of the forty years I spent in education. He asked whether I would draw on my experience and share two words of wisdom. After speaking with him, I realized I had many words of wisdom that could help principals no matter the circumstances in their districts.

Too often the only assistance principals receive comes from a textbook, on-the-job training about their district's agenda, or what they pick up from watching other principals. The reality is that formal guidance culled from books, training, and peers has to be translated into user-friendly tips.

To put it simply, you need wisdom.

Wisdom is the ability to think by drawing on knowledge built up over repeated exposure to certain situations. It is enhanced by new information you seek out over time through training and all the time spent on the job. It culminates in insight that points you toward solutions, resolutions, and actions that address each circumstance with a high degree of authority.

The wisdom in this book is based on decades of academic experience. I started out as a preschool teacher before teaching at the elementary- and middle-school levels. The area superintendent noticed my dedication and my performance results and eventually promoted me to principal of one of the largest elementary schools in that system. For eighteen years I shepherded teachers, students, and staff through the ups and downs any principal finds familiar. Many of my students went on to college and now work in lucrative professions.

When I retired, I worked as an assistant principal at an alternative school and then as a college adjunct teaching early childhood education courses. Finding that work not as rewarding, I went on to work with a Montessori school and then with a chain of daycare centers. Eventually, I landed the position of a clinical supervisor at Brenau University. Through that position, I found my passion assisting teachers and students with maximizing their results.

All those years and experiences led me to create Amyra LLC, a tutorial services company that reaches into schools to propel K–12 students to success. And, of course, I write. After working with a coauthor on a book that lays out the foundation of differentiated instruction, I saw the need to reach out to principals with a dedicated book. *Words of Wisdom for Principals* was born!

This book is divided into sections that broadly group specific types of wisdom into different categories. You'll find sections on your school, your people, and your own position. Each bit of wisdom is defined, the benefits are laid out, and an example is provided. Finally, specific tips are given so that you can make each piece of wisdom work for you.

Feel free to read this book straight through, focus on one section at a time, or open a page at random to discover what waits. Browse through it during school breaks, study it before the academic year begins, or set up sharing groups with other principals to work through the points section by section. No matter how you use this book, you'll add to your own wisdom with every page. You'll become a champion school leader!

Chapter 1

Wisdom for Your School

SHARE RESPONSIBILITIES

Sharing responsibilities is about delegating. Just as one person will struggle to manage a household on their own, a principal will struggle to manage an entire school alone.

Sharing responsibilities is important to how you function and how well your school meets its goals. When you utilize the skills and abilities of your teachers and administrators, you avoid being ensnared by the many details that can obscure the big picture. You become more efficient. Your school becomes more effective. You will also groom others for leadership roles, so your efforts will generate far-reaching opportunities.

Sharing responsibilities can be as simple as allowing individuals to make more decisions within their own area of expertise. It might also come from restructuring the organization chart to shift the chains of command for reporting purposes. As you consider what to delegate, consider which tasks you must perform (like teacher evaluations) and which tasks others must perform (like cross-training other teachers). All other duties are things you should do, things you could do, and things you can do in an emergency. Every one of those intermediary items, like representing the school at off-site meetings, can be performed by others.

Learn to share responsibilities. Identify employees with the skillset that fits one of your tasks. Among those individuals, locate the one with the desire to take on additional responsibility. When you match skills and willingness with an individual you trust, you'll delegate action items that pull your focus away from more important issues.

FOLLOW UP

Following up is the simple act of checking in with people to see whether tasks are on track or to discover the results of completed efforts.

Following up tells your staff that you care about their efforts as well as the results. Every time you check in with someone, you give them the opportunity to ask for assistance or resources. And when you check in after completion, you discover what works for your school and which initiatives require a different approach. Following up allows you to reap what you sow!

Follow up to integrate everyone's efforts into a cohesive, dynamic whole. Check in with new hires soon after they start to emphasize that you care about how they're adjusting. Touching base with teachers who have been around for a while lets them know that you don't take their efforts for granted. Following up with parents who've voiced a concern proves that the entire school puts the students first.

Following up isn't always easy. People who feel that it signals a lack of trust can find it annoying. But if you set the expectation that follow-ups will always occur, you can eliminate that distraction. Follow up with individuals after they've been given a task to see how they're progressing. Check in during the middle of a complicated task or project to help with unexpected issues. And after the project is finished, ask for feedback. Following up will expand your knowledge base, prevent similar issues from recurring, and pinpoint beneficial elements that should be repeated.

FIND OR CREATE AN ANSWER

As a leader, find or create an answer to every inquiry or issue. Finding an answer means drawing on your knowledge or network. Creating an answer results when you use your wisdom to generate unique solutions.

Finding or creating an answer enhances trust. Everyone associated with the school recognizes that the leader will maintain a stable foundation for learning. Principals who find or create answers become role models. They inspire teachers, parents, and even students to search out information, and to utilize creativity and wisdom to generate new solutions.

Finding and creating answers applies to some of the most important issues. When presented with test scores that are slipping, you must first locate relevant information. Are other schools in your region experiencing the same drop? If so, to what degree? If not, how do their procedures differ from your school's procedures? If the answer doesn't appear, you move into creating an answer. What in your previous experience has enhanced students' passion for learning? What has motivated teachers to continue their sterling efforts? What combination of these elements might raise scores?

Finding or creating an answer doesn't mean that you have all the answers at your fingertips. The person in charge of so many areas can't possibly know everything . . . but he or she can, and should, find or create answers with his or her superior resources and knowledge. First, make sure the right questions are being asked. Tap into your network for more information. Focus your team in the right area and then consider the results. Locate the answer or create one from what you've discovered. Finding or creating answers will keep your students and school on the right track.

HELP FAMILIES IN NEED

Helping families in need strengthens the total environment in which your students work and live.

Every step toward helping families in need ensures that every student's home contains the basic necessities required for physical health and psychological stability. Young people who are worried about how much food is in their pantry aren't able to focus fully on their education. The coronavirus epidemic revealed that this situation is far from uncommon. An untold number of families live one paycheck away from not being able to pay their bills or put meals on the table.

For these households, a bag of groceries or a new coat can free up a little breathing room in their monthly budget. Stress in the household goes down, generating a better environment in which to rest and study.

Students are also less likely to feel pressured to find a job that could cut into their study time or even take them out of school.

Different ways to help families in need can be coordinated entirely through the school or in partnership with programs that already serve your community. The food gathered during donation drives, for example, might be picked up by the mail carrier if you collect groceries during the postal service's annual food drive. Winter coats and winter shoes can be collected and sorted by volunteers from your local Goodwill. If your school requires uniforms, be sure to round up unwanted uniforms at the end of each year and offer them to families in need for the following year.

Because your school will always serve families that struggle, plan a year-long campaign that rotates through various types of assistance. Integrate the plan over several years, adding new campaigns each year as the school gains partners through which to work. In the first year, you might plan one assistance activity each semester for a total of two programs. For the second year, you can add two additional activities to cover each half-semester for a total of four programs. You'll raise awareness of the needs of your community while fostering compassion and action among your student body.

ARRIVE EARLY

Arrive early to fresh ideas and you'll build the school of your dreams!

Arriving early is the educator's primary directive. It takes advantage of the best that technology, psychology, and educational research can offer. Arriving early lifts students who are most in need, enhances teacher performance, and keeps kids and adults engaged. It assures parents that their children are receiving the best efforts of their school, and inspires everyone to continue moving forward.

Arriving early has been happening in schools for decades. First, computers replaced paper notebooks. Now tablets are replacing computers. More observations and descriptions have been introduced into science lessons, the amount of individualized reading instruction has increased, and the power of relating lessons to everyday life has been recognized. These innovations have increased the speed of learning and enhanced students' ability to learn.

Arriving early doesn't always involve direct action. Instead, keep abreast of what your network is saying about ideas and innovation. Search your experiences and your wisdom to discover or create initiatives that might be beneficial. Select a single component of that idea to test. If it works, implement the next step. A thoughtful approach and small steps will result in large gains when you arrive early.

PREPARE FOR THE WORST

Preparing for the worst is a form of crisis management that creates a safer, more stable environment.

Preparing for the worst allows you to shepherd students and staff through fires, extreme weather events, and threats of violence. Rather than assuming the worst and allowing fear and anxiety to rule your campus, you maximize safety and security before, during, and after the event. Having clear, logical plans in place assures students, parents, and staff that the many hours they spend at school are safeguarded even if tragedy strikes.

Preparing for the worst is a normal part of any school. Hurricane, tornado, and earthquake procedures exist in regions prone to these kinds of weather events. Every school has fire suppression equipment and evacuation plans. Nowadays, more schools have bomb threat and shooter plans to protect against worst-case scenarios.

Prepare for the worst by reviewing your school's policies and procedures for fire and weather events. Check to see whether your staff is trained in active shooter response methods and visit the Department of Homeland Security website for resources. Prevention is an important component for safety during any event, especially shootings, and the National Institute of Justice is a good place to start. Be sure to plan for follow-up support like counseling for emotional trauma.

TRACK CHANGES

Track changes to keep projects on track, accurately assess results, and enable transparency in reporting and outreach.

When you track changes that occur within and around the school, you grasp a clear understanding of how adjustments made in one area will impact projects and people involved in other areas. The arrival of a large corporation in your city, for example, might attract a new labor force and change the demographics of your student body. A shift in the student body's size or demographics might require more counselors on campus. Roadwork that occurs near your campus could change traffic patterns during drop-off and pickup times.

Although you should follow along as changes are implemented, it's important to keep an eye on upcoming changes, as well. Knowing what's coming down the pike allows you to prepare individuals and procedures for the impact of those changes. And, by notifying those who will be affected ahead of time, you convey the message that everyone plays a part in creating a smooth transition.

Tracking changes goes beyond the initial effects of a change, as well. Even your efforts to manage the ripples caused by new programs might spur the need for changes in areas that are surprisingly far afield. All aspects of a school are interwoven to some degree, and understanding how a shift in one operation modifies another enhances your ability to find success with the new situation. You'll detect potential issues before they gain traction. You'll also discover areas where unexpected successes can be achieved. Since nothing is constant except change, track changes to harness the best and head off the rest.

CREATE A SCHOOL LEADERSHIP TEAM

School leadership teams guide a school's improvement efforts in teaching and learning.

School leadership teams mobilize the commitment of the teachers and parents whose efforts are required for best results. The National Institute for Urban School Improvement found that leadership teams facilitate rapid change, and that those changes are sustained over time. The team also spreads the responsibility for many leadership tasks over a group of individuals, freeing you to focus on the school's overall performance and objectives.

School leadership teams conduct research on educational initiatives and procedures. They help solve problems by providing a wide array of perspectives as well as through ongoing research. They can enhance and expand your existing network as well as that of your teachers. Often they are used to spearhead important but time-consuming initiatives.

Build a school leadership team by inviting staff, parents, and even students to volunteer. Select individuals from every department, grade, community demographic, and skill level to provide the team with a rich pool of resources. Ensure that at least one member understands the school's policies so that he or she can provide guidance on an initiative's likelihood of success. Give the team members a place to gather and task them with setting up their own procedures. Check in with them monthly to see what ideas they've come up with!

BYPASS MONETARY WOES

Bypassing monetary woes means you find ways to enhance the educational experience and learning results through free and low-cost alternatives.

Bypassing monetary woes enhances your school's performance. Rather than worrying so much about how much money you'll receive for each child, you can focus on unique, innovative ways to spur learning. Students become more engaged because they're not facing the same routine. Teachers spark student interest more quickly and are able to utilize more tools in their classrooms. Parents recognize the results of their children's performance because they are more engaged in learning.

Bypassing monetary woes expands on items your school is probably already using. Social media sites are being harnessed to provide updates and class announcements through Twitter and Facebook. E-mail lists for parents allow your school to update parents on school events and changes. Webinars provide professional tips and training for teachers at every level. All these elements are free; at most, some charge small fees for monthly or annual access.

Bypass monetary woes by adding digital tools to your school's arsenal. Engage parents with websites that include 360-degree images from around campus . . . set up by the school's yearbook staff, of course! Provide teachers with lists of podcasts they can download and allow teachers to add to the list. Create a library of downloaded free software students can use to complete school projects. Include video-editing software, audio recording and editing programs, photo-editing software, video game creators, and an in-school chatroom where students can share tips and ask for help.

RESIDE NEAR YOUR SCHOOL ZONE

Residing near your school is a radical concept that places you inside the beating heart of your campus community.

Deciding to reside near your school zone is an excellent investment for principals. Because you are located near the school, you can better understand the lived experiences of your students and their parents. Your on-the-ground view brings you direct information about the challenges and opportunities they face. You'll be able to pull more people, including those who don't have school-aged children, into the quest for effective education.

Principals who reside near their schools truly own the wants and needs of the campus community. Every time you go home or participate in events outside the school, you'll explore the conditions that surround, and therefore impact, academic success. You'll see firsthand the obstacles that might interfere with students' ability to understand and absorb the curriculum. As you meet more people and make more friends, your network will grow exponentially more quickly than if you lived farther away. This stronger and broader network provides you with important resources to tackle longstanding problems as well as new issues.

Residing near your school also helps you recognize the struggles parents might face as they reach for a life that supports learning. The same issues that impact them will have an effect on your own household. The work you perform to build a better life for yourself will also benefit your neighbors and your school. Simple neighborly acts like giving away extra vegetables you've grown or swapping home maintenance tips puts you in a position to help other families achieve a higher quality of daily living. With every wave good morning, you'll strengthen ties between your school and the campus community.

Residing near your school zone is an intense commitment. The interpersonal connections derived from casual contact with your campus community builds a strong foundation for education. Personal activities from grocery shopping to membership in social groups will expand your network. Your ability to see both challenges and opportunities as they arise empowers you to act quickly and decisively. Your pool of resources will grow deeper and richer. On a personal and professional level, living near your campus will give you and the families you serve richly satisfying rewards.

MAKE HEALTHY CHOICES

Making healthy choices means every decision is driven by the desire to enhance the school, improve learning, and create a positive, beneficial environment.

Make healthy choices to create a strong educational foundation. Every decision should improve the performance of your teachers, enable students to achieve, and drive the school to successfully achieve its goals. Healthy choices enhance the physical and mental well-being of everyone on campus. They create an environment that is safe, supportive, and nurturing for young minds as well as career professionals.

Healthy choices are nowhere more important than with school rankings. While it's true that test scores are a critical component, many other factors are also tabulated. The profile of your school (how your school presents itself) is an important part of the comparison. Statistics on attendance, graduation rates, violent incidences, and other data also count. Even the reviews that parents write are used these days. When you work on every front to make healthy choices, every decision will impact where your school lands in the ranks.

Healthy choices come in a variety of forms. Most people think of the healthy food initiatives sweeping school cafeterias, and this is certainly one type of healthy choice. Beyond that, emotional well-being can be supported with counselors and peer groups where individuals can discuss their issues. Academic fitness can be enhanced through study groups, in-school chat rooms dedicated to specific subjects, and afterschool programs. Make healthy choices to supercharge your school's fitness!

CLIMATE CHANGE CHALLENGE

Ramp your school up for a climate change challenge to encourage students to advocate for our planet.

When you set a climate change challenge for your school, you'll provide opportunities for more than the planet. You'll also empower students to take decisive action on an issue that, while it affects all of us, will significantly impact their generation. In meeting the school's challenge, students will learn how to work together in a group that will attract young people from different backgrounds. Finally, students will learn advocacy skills that will serve them throughout their lives.

Encourage students to join a climate change challenge afterschool group. Throughout the year, they can track scientific findings related to climate change and the efforts made by organizations and nations to address it. The group can distribute their findings to the entire school through posters, brief weekly additions to the morning announcements, or through a monthly newsletter they write and produce. Annual outings can visit local businesses or organizations that can demonstrate how their climate change initiatives work.

The climate change challenge students can spur others to participate even if they don't join the group. Climate-related outreach, including artwork, posters, songs and videos, can be distributed throughout the campus and posted to the school's social media. Students could hold a "bike drive" to encourage commuters to ride bikes or take public transportation. They can encourage anyone to stop by their meetings to listen in or ask questions. Having peers provide information raises the level of trust felt by curious students, so the impact will be strong.

Advocacy can reach beyond your educational community. The group can spearhead a petition supporting specific actions and collect signatures. The petition, with a letter explaining the reasons why the group supports a specific action or actions, can be sent to legislators. During election cycles, they can provide information to the community about candidates' climate change track records. The research, outreach, and energy that goes into these efforts will enhance their communication and writing skills. Through this process, they'll become more engaged citizens.

BEGIN EACH DAY ANEW

Begin each day anew is, in the words of Ralph Waldo Emerson, the ability to "Write it on your heart/that every day is the best day in the year."

Beginning each day anew allows you to move past yesterday. Begin each day knowing that how you spend these hours creates your future. It allows you to switch gears, to ramp up with fresh effort, to reengage your passion. Beginning each day anew is a powerful motivator!

Beginning each day anew works for your school. Whatever last year's test scores were, on this day, they can rise. Students whose home lives are mired in negative circumstances can arrive on campus with every reason to believe in themselves. Teachers who faced challenges before can start down new roads and engage fully with their faith in the importance of education. Parents disappointed by grades or attitudes can join hands in creating a brighter today for their children.

Begin each day anew before you set foot on campus. Today is a blank slate on which you can write, draw, doodle, or paint anything you wish. Select three things you'd like to accomplish and then move them to the center of your desk. Throughout the day, make sure you're moving forward at least a little on all three. At the end of the day, tuck away that colorful slate knowing you have fulfilled your vision to the best of your ability. Get up the next morning and do it all anew!

WELCOME FAILURE

Welcoming failure means that you provide the space and time for people to try new things.

Welcome failure to encourage innovation and exploration. When your staff is free to experiment with new ideas, they'll fail more often than they'll succeed. Failure is an important part of the path forward: it encourages new ideas while supporting the talented, passionate individuals who care enough to put extra effort into bringing those ideas to life.

Welcoming failure expands the tools that are available to teachers, students, and staff. New ideas are almost always expected to provide exceptionally greater benefits than current tools or procedures. When the idea fails to yield exceptional results, yet provides the same benefits as the current method, you have found a new tool. Only by failing to achieve a lofty goal have you discovered a unique and useful tool!

Welcome failure at every level. Let students start afterschool programs, work together with other classes, or even join forces with other grade levels for certain projects. Provide teachers with the open, accepting environment that spurs creative thinking. Encourage service personnel to implement new techniques on a trial basis. Give parents a school-hosted internet forum in which to share thoughts about new programs they can spearhead. Welcome failure at every level and improve every aspect of your school!

SANITATION

The coronavirus pandemic demonstrated just how critical sanitation is to our public spaces, and schools are at the top of that list. In addition to the usual need for clean drinking fountains and properly supplied restrooms, the likelihood of facing future health issues means that schools should continue some covid-based practices to keep students healthy and safe. Your school should also be ready at any moment to implement full-scale health safety procedures.

One element of sanitation that has proven important is ventilation. Simple steps like having cleaning crews open windows while they're working inside a classroom can help older schools increase their airflow. For buildings with windows that don't open, consider propping entrances open for a quarter of an hour as students arrive. Allowing fresh air to flow through the halls changes out stagnant air and increases ventilation during the period when students are crowded together.

Other sanitation steps that were brought in during covid should become a permanent part of the school's operations. Supply all restrooms with signs encouraging handwashing. Save money by skipping the antibacterial soap; plenty of studies show that regular soap is just as effective. Ensure that trash receptacles are available in all classrooms, at intersections where hallways meet, and in gyms and cafeterias. Schedule additional rubbish collection rounds if necessary. Keep a supply of masks on hand for use by any staff or student.

Cut costs associated with these additional sanitation measures by pulling students into the mix. Get the afterschool art group to create handwashing signs for the restrooms. Offer a free lunch once a week to any student who uses their lunch period to empty the trashcans that tend to overflow before the end of the day. Have students make their own masks using simple directions downloaded from the internet, and then store these in homeroom classrooms or other central locations. In addition to keeping everyone at school safe, you'll get more buy-in by involving the very population you're looking to protect.

ALIGN GOALS

Align goals to ensure that everyone at your school owns the school's goals.

Aligning goals allows you to execute new ideas more quickly. When everyone from students to staff agrees, existing policies and procedures are valued and are implemented more efficiently. Importantly, goals aligned across your entire school allow you to lead with far less friction.

Align goals with every organization that comes into contact with the students, teachers, or school. A partnership between families, community members, and your school provides broader resources. Sharing rights and responsibilities creates partnerships based on the strengths of each group and your school. The result of any effort will be an increase in the quality of the educational experience as well as long-term benefits to the community.

Align goals by beginning every initiative with a review of how the project will meet specific school goals. This outlines your expectations for the project and clarifies how to document progress. When you align goals, selecting individuals who demonstrate particular strengths will be easier. Participants who understand how goals align manage their tasks more efficiently, focus their efforts on elements that will move the project forward, and understand why their effort is important. Align goals to supercharge your school's success!

SAFEGUARD THE MONEY

Safeguard the money to protect taxpayer funds or funds raised locally to support your school.

Safeguarding the money ensures that funding is available when you need it. As principal, you must maintain a working knowledge of where the money for your school is going. In instances where funds have been misappropriated, mistrust and innuendos linger among staff and in the community long after the issue has been addressed. Build the atmosphere you want in your school by keeping tabs on every dollar!

Safeguarding the money keeps your school functioning smoothly. In instances where funds were misappropriated, employees have been interviewed, transferred, dismissed . . . even arrested. In Maryland, an audit revealed that federal stimulus and Title I money was used on dinner cruises, and inappropriate amounts were spent on other entertainment events. Lawmakers immediately called for a more expansive review of the entire school system. The headaches involved for innocent staff are not something any principal wants to experience.

Safeguard the money first and foremost by placing the school's accounts into the hands of a trusted bookkeeper or secretary who will not compromise their job for greed or a prison number. If money goes missing, the law clearly states that it must be reported immediately. Once the situation has been thoroughly investigated and resolved, corrective actions such as quarterly audits should be conducted. The increased auditing will catch discrepancies related to mismanagement or outright theft before they cause real harm to your school and its reputation.

FOSTER THE GRANDS

Foster the grands to turn attention toward segments of the community that could use a little extra attention while opening opportunities for intergenerational learning.

Fostering grands puts a spotlight on elder-care homes and assisted living facilities. Individuals who live and work in these situations have a lot to offer younger generations. When relationships are built across the age gap, participants on both sides learn new perspectives. They discover different ways to live. The exchange might inspire them to adjust something about themselves, to think deeply about who they are and what they want to become. Considering that the pace of change has only sped up during the previous century, disparate generations really do have a lot to share.

To achieve the best results when fostering grands, the staff member who will head up the efforts should connect with local facilities and organizations that serve elderly populations. Discuss the needs of each organization's demographic to pinpoint areas where students of different ages can help out. Younger students might offer to read their favorite books out loud or share their favorite show-and-tell items. Since these types of activities can be conducted through video chats, students don't need to leave the school. By connecting digitally, they can regularly visit with elders and build truly meaningful relationships.

Older students could help individuals or groups by walking them through ways to use different apps, shop online, or access their e-mail. During video meetings, students might present skits or discuss articles in the local paper they found interesting. At least some of the meetings can have an open format during which the students talk about the modern things that worry them. The elders can respond with how they might approach the issue. Over time, these exchanges have the potential to develop into friendships. Fostering grands will foster the best in your school as well as your community.

SCHEDULE CHECKUPS

Scheduling checkups means checking in on various important components regularly.

Scheduling checkups allows you to check in on how well things are operating. You can assess performance, efficiency, and the school's climate through much less formal procedures than those demanded by state and federal procedures. The informality of the process often encourages candor, allowing you to locate and address issues long before they get out of control.

One important example of scheduling checkups is the information garnered from students. A survey can reveal issues visible only to the kids. A culture of bullying revolving around certain activities can come to light when multiple individuals report harassment. Importantly, checkups can provide measurable statistics on the results achieved by corrective action.

Schedule checkups with staff, students, and parents. Utilize a short survey tailored for each group. Allow individuals to fill them out anonymously to ensure complete confidence and honest responses. After the results have been tabulated, share them with the group. Provide your own comments and ask for feedback! Then address any issues. In later checkups, include questions that ask for participants' views on the results.

CREATE GUIDEBOOKS

Creating guidebooks allows you to disseminate the wisdom you've gathered—and the decades of wisdom embedded in your staff—to individuals who need advice.

Creating guidebooks allows you to speak on a more personal basis with everyone at your school. Guidebooks that blend lists of resources with tips, inspirational quotes, and anecdotes from others can become popular reference guides for everyday school life. For most of your staff, their careers are more than jobs . . . and for students; education is the foundation for their lives. Creating guidebooks provides a unique opportunity to touch individuals where they are as well as impact their future.

Creating guidebooks is a valuable service for teachers, students, and parents. A student guidebook can offer advice on everything from effective study techniques to resources for those who are depressed. The teacher's version should encourage developmental opportunities with descriptions of workshops by individuals who have attended, while parent guidebooks can help them navigate everything from scheduling to homework.

Create guidebooks with inputs from the different target groups. Ask students from higher grade levels to provide their best advice for kids at lower grade levels. Encourage teachers to submit anecdotes about how they've resolved issues as well as inspirational moments. Ask parents to share their best coping tips with other parents, and make sure teachers get to sound off on the best ways parents can help their students. Include quotes from different individuals to make the guidebooks as popular as they are useful!

FUEL YOUR SCHOOL

Be creative in the face of budget cuts to fuel your school.

Fueling your school is a necessary part of every principal's job. New equipment, office supplies, books, and class materials feed the hungry minds in your care. Providing students and teachers with the proper resources allows their focus to remain on exploring and learning. The last thing any principal wants to do is turn down a new idea because the funding just isn't there.

Fueling your school has immediate and long-term impacts. In the short run, individuals are given the resources to explore new ideas and innovative processes. Over the long term, adequate funding creates stability in the learning environment. The overarching result is that student outcomes meet or exceed expectations . . . the only result that really matters.

Rather than relying only on the usual sources every school in your district competes for, find creative ways to fuel your school. Connect with nonprofits like literary magazines or history museums that might send staff members to your school for a weeklong program. If you hear that a company is remodeling a department or upgrading their electronics, ask whether they'll donate the old employee tablets, computers, or furniture. If these items aren't useful for your school, schedule a year-end rummage sale to raise funds. No matter what opportunity you spy, never be afraid to ask . . . and always ask for more than you think you'll get. You might be surprised by the results!

TRANSFORM LOW PERFORMERS

When you transform low performers, you hand educators the power to attend to the needs of the new students who arrive in their classrooms each year.

Every school has to deal with students who aren't meeting their true potential. Transform low performers by finding ways to offer frequent tutoring to students. Determine the type of specialized support required by an individual, and then channel intensive support from counselors, peer groups, or parent volunteers. Doing so builds a culture based on high expectations at every level of achievement. When the environment is geared toward lifting every student, you'll reach more of the student body and build a better school.

Tap into the resources available for transforming low performers. Press the district to reallocate funds based on student needs. Aggressively recruit teachers who express the desire to engage in this rewarding work. Use newsletters, outreach opportunities, and word of mouth to spread information among parents about your mission. Ask them for resources they might know about, and keep the door open for volunteers interested in lifting students to their fullest potential.

When you transform low performers, you impact your school as well as your community. More eyes will turn toward your school. With that added attention come a host of benefits. You'll discover that people from outside the educational field will approach you with ideas and offers of support. Your school will become the place where parents want to send their children. Your students will own their own potential and will rise to new heights. Making opportunities for excellence accessible to every learner creates its own vortex of energy, validation, and results.

APPEARANCES COUNT!

Appearances count recognizes that everything about your school conveys a message about you, your teachers, your students, and your place in the community.

Appearances count is a message your school might convey through dress codes or uniforms. More so, though, this wisdom encompasses the broader way you present to the community. A professional appearance makes students, parents, and staff comfortable with the school and each other. Those positive impressions encourage everyone to focus on educational achievements.

Appearances count has an impact through the smallest of gestures. The cleanliness of the hallways conveys that your facility is well maintained and safe. Enforcing tardiness rules showcases one part of the procedures that keep things running smoothly day by day. Quick responses to student and parental concerns prove that they are in capable hands. Clear communications with your teachers prove they can trust their leader.

Advance the idea that appearances count with students and staff. If you see an empty water bottle on the floor, pick it up yourself. If you see someone else doing the same, thank them! Sponsor a cleanup day for the roadside fronting your school with students and parents. Set aside a small area in front of the school where anyone can bring a plant one day a year, and mark each plant with the donor's name. If some of them can be used in the science class, even better! You'll enhance personal responsibility, school pride, and academic performance with the same effort.

CHAMPION CHALLENGES

Championing challenges means that you welcome challenges as a way to become a champion yourself!

Champion challenges to make champions of the individuals who overcome those challenges. Whenever you champion a challenge, you tell people that you care. More so, you prove to them that they have your attention as individuals. Whether it's a student or a teacher, a parent or a fellow principal, help them see that overcoming a challenge makes them a champion.

Champion challenges even if they seem overwhelming. You might discover that your budget isn't going to allow for an important annual event to take place. Champion the challenge by alerting others to the shortfall. Rather than seeking funding, ask for alternate ways to host the event. It might be as simple as getting students to agree to a smaller activity that fits the budget. The solution could be as complex as having students approach local businesses for donations of food or supplies. When you champion the event, you champion a solution!

Champion challenges with creativity and compassion. Creative ideas resolve issues. Call on individuals inside and outside the school. Garner the creativity of the masses to find the best solution. Throughout the process, have compassion for those who will be disappointed by the challenge itself. Help them understand that facing the challenge will make them stronger. And of course, champion your own challenges. Your school will become its own champion!

HEAL THE HURT

Healing the hurt moves your school community through the worst of times.

Heal the hurt to ensure that major tragedies—the accident or depression that takes a life, the horror of a school shooting, or debilitating illness—do not inflict any pain that can possibly be prevented. It allows your school, and the lives of the people involved, to get back to something like a normal life after the healing process called grieving.

Even if you're brand new to the job of a principal, you hardly need any examples of times where you'll need to heal the hurt. The media keeps our nation informed . . . sometimes too much so . . . about every new attack that occurs on school grounds. What you might not realize, though, is that the school community also needs time to grieve when a student or teacher falls ill. The recognition that the person is losing their quality of life or will eventually die must be recognized so that it can be mourned.

To heal the hurt, be prepared long before a crisis occurs. Ensure that your counselors and even your teachers understand how to interact with students who have just witnessed or been involved in a traumatic event. Afterward, let students know what changes will be implemented to ensure that they can get the help they might need as individuals or as a group. Share that same information with the entire community. Provide your staff with time to work out their own grief as a group of adults. When it's appropriate, hold sessions for the parents as well.

ADOPT A NEIGHBORHOOD

When students adopt a neighborhood from their community, they actively participate in civic responsibility while changing lives.

The steps needed to adopt a neighborhood are relatively simple, but the payoffs are large. Students will feel more engaged with their neighbors and the people who form their communities. Individuals from the targeted areas, as well as the surrounding areas, will celebrate the young people who care enough to help others where they live and work. If the program teams up with public service organizations for specific events, the effort has the potential to become a recurring annual event that maximizes the impact.

Getting started is as easy as heading into neighborhoods near the campus to pick up trash. Blend this outing with the school's climate challenge or environmental awareness efforts by sorting trash into recycling containers. If a public park is within walking distance, call the local government and arrange for the students to sweep pathways or rake leaves. Beautify adopted areas by wrapping lampposts with paintings students create, cozies they knit, or other textile creations. To ramp up the beautification with social interactions, have the students draw on sidewalks with chalk, or they can paint abstract designs on telephone poles with nontoxic, water-based colors that will wash off with the next rain.

Utilize technology to extend the effort further. Students can post to neighborhood-based social sharing sites like NextDoor.com to encourage year-round cleanup efforts by locals. A contest for the cleanest sidewalk or prettiest garden can be run by the adopt a neighborhood group. The students will be responsible for outreach, judging pictures sent in by contestants, and designing the certificate given to the winner. A few months before the holidays, students can run a gift drive for items to be left on the doorsteps of every home on a specific block.

When your students adopt a neighborhood, they deepen their commitment to their local communities. They improve the quality of life for neighborhoods that might otherwise never have access to anything better. The addition of creative ideas, like beautification through arts and crafts, adds an element of fun that will open hearts and minds to your school and among your students.

MOVE FORWARD

Move forward means that you focus on doing—that your school is constantly engaged in proactive efforts that will enhance and improve performance and operations.

Moving forward prevents stagnation. Workplaces, hospitals, and other areas where people spend a significant period of time have found that even small changes in the environment improve morale and enhance performance. When your staff and students know that the school is a living, active institution, they feel good about being there every day.

Moving forward can happen in any area of a school. Every time students implement a fundraising effort, they are advancing projects that will have an impact beyond their individual group. Teachers who engage in development programs advance their abilities and skills. Parents who spearhead in-school or afterschool efforts advance the programs as well as school-wide engagement.

Move forward by creating transformation zones in your school. Task each department with one area in which they will improve during the academic year. As progress is made, update the entire school about milestones. Take the opportunity to discuss challenges each zone faces so that help can arrive from outside those departments. Celebrate the achievements for each transformational zone at the end of the year and move your entire school forward!

REASSESS AND REPAIR

Reassess and repair allows you to approach recurring issues with a clear mind that is free of frustration.

Reassess and repair is an attitude that emphasizes solutions . . . even when you thought an issue had been resolved. The approach assures staff and students that their leader is dedicated to resolving challenges fully and completely. You'll allow your school to adapt to new circumstances and create the flexibility to revisit elements that need to be adjusted to achieve greater performance.

Reassess and repair is immensely valuable with your people. Students who backslide in behavioral patterns can be caught before they cause real problems for others or themselves. When backsliding comes to light, you reassess the original situation to ensure that everything was done that could be done. Then you consider how the current situation is similar to and different from prior circumstances. Finally, you implement whatever repairs are needed to the original steps to create change.

Reassess and repair can be used even in areas where performance is strong. Reassess ongoing efforts to determine how well they are succeeding. Apply those steps to other projects to enhance their performance. Whenever you discover an area that is working well but could work better, repair the weaknesses by making adjustments as required. Reassess and repair and then reap the rewards!

EFFECTIVE SECURITY

Effective security measures lock down the safety of the school, its property and, most importantly, its people.

Schools have always been considered safe havens where children from every socioeconomic level and identity can reap the benefits of an education. Now more than ever, attention to effective security on campus is a must. Instead of relying solely on expensive measures, explore creative ways to layer new safety options atop existing protocols.

Start with one of your greatest resources, your people. Communicate to your teachers, your parents, and even your students that they are part of the security team working at your school. If someone sees an individual on campus they don't recognize or who isn't displaying a school-issued ID, they should report the sighting immediately. Make this easy by providing a number or e-mail that is used only for reporting security issues via call, text, or e-mail. Ask a student tech group or computer science class to build a security app that provides messaging, photo, and video functions. Test the effectiveness of your messaging by asking an adult you trust to walk through the halls one day between classes and note how quickly reports come in.

If controlling access to the building by keeping doors locked isn't possible, implement a blended system. Make sure that someone on the staff is patrolling the halls between and during every class. Maintain equipment like cameras and monitors regularly, and find ways to implement temporary coverage when equipment is down for more than a short time. Prevention is always the best form of defense.

Plan ahead in case your school faces a crisis. Provide each room with blackout curtains or similar heavy fabric outfitted with suction cups to quickly block out windows. Place whistles or similar devices in every classroom to serve as emergency calls when individuals cannot leave their rooms. Even if cellphones are banned in your classrooms, ensure that every teacher keeps one in an unlocked desk drawer for emergency calls. Simple, inexpensive steps can save priceless lives.

TWEAK THE TONE

Tweaking the tone is an ongoing effort to maintain the goals you set at the beginning of the academic year. It's like a tune-up for your school!

Tweaking the tone keeps your annual goals on track. The expectations you laid out at the beginning of the year—for students, parents and staff—will be nudged back on track through small efforts. The energy involved in minor tweaks over time is far less than the big push required to shift something that has gone awry close to the deadline.

Tweaking the tone is all about enhancing enthusiasm. The atmosphere of your school should be healthy, proactive, and encouraging. The atmosphere can't be created with an individual program; instead, the atmosphere is generated at the beginning of the academic year and then kept alive by frequent updates and reminders.

Often you'll find that you must tweak the tone in specific departments or on individual projects. Once you've set the atmosphere for the entire school, your ongoing dedication and daily efforts support the overall atmosphere. But for efforts where you're not involved daily, check in occasionally to monitor the tone. A group that is frustrated by minimal resources can be spurred by your enthusiasm and gratitude. A program being waylaid by an uncooperative or difficult individual can be reinvigorated after a short chat with that individual. Tweak the tone to keep your school on target throughout the year!

PROFESSIONAL PEN PALS

Professional pen pals enhance your school's network—the individuals and organizations who can assist and support your efforts.

Professional pen pals offer a simple yet effective way to encourage students to consider different career choices with insider information into what different jobs demand. They allow your teachers to connect with professionals who are interested in supporting education but who might not have children at your school. Finally, professional pen pals expand your network of individuals and organizations.

Professional pen pals enhance diversity. A history class might write a group letter to a single elder-care facility. The class can pose questions about certain time periods that will be covered in the curriculum. Then, when that unit is covered, the residents' responses can be read aloud. The personal stories will add depth to what students learn. If the class can visit the facility for an hour or a day, or if the facility can bring the participants to the class, the experience takes on even more meaning!

Professional pen pals can be developed at every level. Different classrooms can reach out to local museums and other nonprofits that focus on areas tied to the curriculum. Teachers can be pen pals with local businesses that might donate a small percentage of revenues from sales to support fundraising. Your pen pals might include nonprofits, news reporters, or others who want to support educational efforts. Keep the effort simple; one letter exchange every month is enough to spark new ideas and new connections.

REFORM THE RULES

Reforming the rules allows your school to work within the guidelines without being suffocated.

Reforming the rules recognizes that your school operates under a host of federal and state regulations. Within those guidelines, however, you can create more freedom. Reforming the rules allows you to adjust the details of how those regulations are met so that teachers, students, and staff can be comfortable and innovative.

Reforming the rules can help you meet one of the most difficult goals, the testing standards. Although your teachers have to ensure that students meet those standards, you actually have a lot of leeway inside the classrooms. Look into methodologies like differentiated instruction to enhance academic performance, and you'll reform the rules for the greatest good.

Reform the rules with thoughtfulness and creativity. Your reformations are only the first step. Encourage your teachers to reform the rules . . . always with your guidance, of course . . . within their classrooms. Allow them to negotiate the changing terrain when they meet their new students. Encourage them to adapt as their students change during the academic year. Reform the rules to encourage individuals to brainstorm, create, and keep on track!

COMPREHENSIVE CARE

Comprehensive care is a student-run effort to assist a single family (or a handful of families) over the course of the school year.

When students participate in a comprehensive care program, they achieve direct, personal experience with how small efforts can generate big changes in the lives of others. This close-up experience shows them the kinds of daily struggles others go through while providing a way to help. Students who work with families with children will feel grateful that they are lucky enough to be able to help. Because their activities will reward them with a sense of pride, they'll be more likely to reach out to other students who need help with homework or who just need to see a friendly smile.

Families who wish to be part of the comprehensive care program can provide wish lists at the start of the school year. Create an information sheet with examples of the types of requests students might fulfill, such as light housekeeping chores, light yard work, or donations of school supplies or clothing. Leave a space free for the family to write in other requests. You might discover that an adult member wants help writing a resume, or that one of their children is being bullied so much they'd like someone to walk them home.

Volunteer efforts associated with comprehensive care often ramp up around the holidays. Be sure to keep families who need assistance in view throughout the year. Winters can be difficult for seasonal workers, so run a food drive before winter begins. A family expecting a new baby could benefit from a month-long effort to gather donations of diapers, baby food, and infant clothing. "Beauty Baskets" filled with basic supplies like toilet paper, tissues, liquid soap and soap bars, and toothpaste and toothbrushes can plug gaps in the budget any time of the year.

The best thing about comprehensive care is that it is limited only by the abilities of the student body to respond. Consider, too, that the requests your school is unable to fulfill might be met if students refer the family to other organizations, so be sure they create and update a list of appropriate agencies categorized by focus. Mental health and wellness counseling, food stamp and WIC programs, homeless shelters, domestic abuse shelters, and suicide prevention programs should be included on the list. No matter how little or how much your school's program offers, the help it provides will be welcome.

REDUCE RECIDIVISM

Reducing recidivism focuses attention on reducing the number of students retained at a grade level.

Reduce recidivism to reduce behavioral problems with students who are held back a year. You'll stave off the nearly inevitable problems that occur two to three years later when the gains of retention fade. You'll eliminate the self-esteem issues that result when the student begins to fail again. You'll create better future possibilities for students, and reduce the amount of time needed to address problems.

Reducing recidivism potentially has its greatest impact with learning-disabled students. Most struggle with achievement tests that ask them to concentrate for long periods, work on their own, and continue working after facing material they find difficult to understand. Ensure that the benchmarks applied to student learning relate to test standards. Offer tutors and call on peers the students trust for help. You'll prepare those students for the rigors of testing and reduce their incidents of retention.

Reduce recidivism by exploring options. For some students, tutoring or assistance from formal or informal peer groups might prevent retention. For others, counseling or other types of emotional support will be the intervention that's truly needed. Still others might need extracurricular activities to enhance their confidence and thereby improve academic motivation. When you reduce recidivism, you prevent students from paying a price for years to come.

STRENGTHEN STRENGTH

Strengthening strength focuses your school on the best it has to offer!

Strengthening strength allows you to focus on what works best. It prevents you from wasting time on things that are less effective. When you turn more attention to strengths than to weaknesses, you create an atmosphere in which weaknesses are addressed by the things your school does well. You expend less effort, your teachers perform better, and your students are less frustrated.

Strengthen strengths in your students to enhance motivation and performance. When high school students receive feedback from teachers on their strengths, the students have significantly lower rates of tardiness and absenteeism. They also have higher GPAs. These kinds of results can be seen after only one semester, making it a powerful and easy way to improve your school!

Strengthen strengths using strength assessment tests. Gallup's Strengths Explorer targets grades 6 through 10. Workuno offers a free strengths test online that can help teachers and staff recognize their top abilities. When individuals recognize their own strengths, they can focus on developing those areas more. When others are aware of those strengths, they can call on high performers to meet goals and tackle challenges as they arise.

DEVICES IN CLASSROOMS

The understanding of devices in classrooms has changed a lot over the years. Allowing students to use personal cellphones and laptops, and allowing internet access during class periods can, when thoughtfully integrated, provide educational benefits.

One of the biggest factors behind considering devices in classrooms is that today's students are true digital natives. From the time they're old enough to lift a finger, they've been using touchscreens and remotes to control and explore their world. Their comfort and familiarity with electronics can make exploring new ideas much less daunting. You'll be using something that is already present in every aspect of their lives to enhance their education.

Adding cellphone and computer use to lessons provides a host of advantages for educators. Communication of everything from assignments, supplementary materials, and scheduling becomes much easier. Educators will be able to assign group projects more frequently because these digital natives prefer to share and collaborate through their devices. And, of course, updates from the administrative side can be sent directly to student's phones or e-mails, which speeds the spread of information.

Wise use of devices includes implementing some basic guidelines. Requiring devices to be put away (stored out of sight) when not in use will help students stay on task. Schools that provide internet service can limit the types of websites that can be accessed through their connection.

Classrooms with seating configured in clusters or groups, rather than the traditional rows, allow teachers to easily monitor device usage.

To encourage compliance, students who refuse to follow the guidelines can be required to complete assignments offline in class or at home on their own time. Head off problems by encouraging digital citizenship with discussions about the appropriate use of devices in different situations, including those that occur off campus. Using one of the top skill sets held by many of today's students will hold their attention and support their success.

SURVIVE THEN THRIVE

Surviving then thriving gets you through a crisis in a way that moves you beyond the crisis with strength.

Surviving then thriving provides you with the determination needed to soldier through the most disruptive issues. You reduce the amount of damage incurred and then quickly regroup and rebuild. In some cases, you'll discover that the disruption allows you to rebuild in ways that turn the challenge into something positive.

Surviving then thriving allows you to excel during challenges that might otherwise cripple the school. The tragedy at Ferguson is a prime example. During the dangerous protests, children and parents found it difficult to penetrate crowds while traveling to and from school. Volunteers from the community reduced the impact of the protests on the community and the school.

Survive then thrive by doing whatever is necessary to get everyone through a crisis. Utilize your network and creative ideas to shepherd your people through the worst. Then engage everyone in discussions of the event. Ask what could have been done differently and share stories of what worked. You'll prove that your school is a stable, safe place no matter what's going on.

REFRESH AND RECHARGE

Refreshing and recharging ensures that morale stays high.

Refreshing and recharging ensures that you and your staff—and even your students—are psychologically prepared to give it their all. You and your staff become more enthusiastic. Challenges don't seem so overwhelming. Students are motivated to reach for higher goals. Even parents benefit because happy students and positive teachers resonate in every contact they have with the school.

Refresh and recharge your workers to enhance loyalty and reduce turnover. Companies with large numbers of unhappy employees suffer higher absenteeism rates and much higher employee turnover; the same impact will be found at your school. When you refresh and recharge your people, you create a more stable environment for students, reduce the cost of addressing issues, and retain strong performers for longer periods.

Refresh and recharge with little gestures that mean a lot. Deposit a batch of donuts in the teacher break room on random days. Reverse trick-or-treat on Halloween by visiting classrooms to hand out pencils to the students. Invite your staff to a potluck on the football field one Friday during lunch. Set up a quick mix-and-mingle so that parents and teachers can get to know each other on a less formal basis. Your efforts will refresh and recharge your school!

ENGAGE WITH THE ENVIRONMENT

Engaging with the environment sets up an eco-conscious facility that generates higher morale and saves money.

Engaging with the environment gives you new ways to publicize positive elements of your school. An eco-conscious campus makes students and staff feel good because their school activities won't negatively impact the environment. Because you'll reduce the amount of energy, water, and materials used, your budget becomes easier to manage!

Engaging with the environment is changing schools across the nation. One school in Kentucky uses rainwater to flush their toilets. Another in New York installed solar panels, while the transportation facility for schools in Virginia Beach features wind turbines. In 2011, Maryland became the first state to legislate that students must become environmentally literate before graduation. Any efforts you make today could take you a step closer to meeting your own state's laws if they ever adopt similar rules.

Engage with the environment through low-cost efforts. Place recycling bins in every classroom to collect cans and paper. Consider using separate trash containers in the cafeteria for food scraps that can be composted. Set the thermostat at 68 degrees in winter and 78 degrees during warmer seasons. When you're considering a larger project like solar panels or water use, turn to government and nonprofit grants for funding.

RESCUE A SHELTER

Because kids and pets are a natural fit, let your school *r*escue a shelter. Students who participate will exercise organizational skills while developing compassion.

Rescuing a shelter is a popular idea that is bound to meet success in your district. Students who gather together for this effort can reach out on their campus as well as to the local community. Thinking about how the different items will be utilized conveys a better understanding of the challenges of caring for a pet. Because students will be developing their ability to feel empathy, they'll be better able to reach out to fellow students in a caring, kind manner.

Animal shelters are constantly in need of certain items. Old towels keep the critters and the facilities clean. Old blankets provide bedding that doesn't cost the shelter anything. Unopened pet food and treats are a big part of their budget, so donations are always appreciated. Paper towels and cleaning supplies, including scrub brushes and rubber gloves, are another high-demand area. Pet toys, leashes, grooming supplies, and flea and tick medicines will keep the animals happy and healthy. Office supplies like reams of paper and pens are always appreciated.

When the donations are ready for delivery, consider adding in other efforts to rescue the shelter. The day the group drops off the supplies, schedule a tour of the shelter. While the group is on site, they can clean out cages, change the bedding, walk the dogs, and play with the cats. If an outing is too much to organize, ask the shelter to bring a few friendly rescues to the school when they pick everything up. The rescue group can meet the animals and the staff they're helping.

After the donations have been sent, the group can set up additional efforts to rescue a shelter. They can advise other schools on the best way to set up a program in their own area. Students who have pets at home can provide basic animal training tips to other students, teach new pet owners the best way to groom their animals, and provide checklists of vaccinations and other exams animals should have early in life. In areas where the county requires pets to be registered, a fundraiser can help individuals in need pay the fees. The group's continuous activity will give your entire school a wonderful way to work together.

GRADE YOUR GRADUATES

Grading your graduates tracks students as they move through their lives to prove your school's lifelong impact.

Grading your graduates allows you to meet the needs of your community. Tracking information about students after they've graduated provides real, quantifiable evidence of your school's effectiveness. When graduates succeed in life, the parents of current students know their children are in good hands. Today's students can look forward to a bright tomorrow!

Grading graduates was actively pursued with 55 high schools by a nonprofit called Big Picture Company. Over the course of 12 years, graduates were followed to measure postsecondary degree attainment, career milestones, relationships, civic involvement, and happiness. The information guided the participating schools in staff development, operational policies, and so much more!

Grade your graduates with simple steps. Engage them on Facebook or other social media where Big Picture found engagement to be highest. Invite them to participate in surveys you can set up for free through sites like SurveyMonkey. Ask about college plans, paid jobs, living situations, and relationships with parents, friends, partners, and children. Since the principal's participation was critical to gathering data, let your graduates know you support these efforts. Grade schools can implement the same sort of tracking when their population graduates to high school!

ENHANCE EMOTIONAL EDUCATION

Enhance emotional education to generate a balanced, healthy atmosphere in which learning can take place.

Enhancing emotional education boosts academic achievement by 11 percent in most student populations. For individuals classified as at-risk, academic achievement can be enhanced 17 percent. Social-emotional learning also reduces the human and financial costs of violent behavior and addiction.

Enhancing emotional education is probably something you're already doing. Every program that reduces instances of bullying, addresses addiction, and prevents violence allows social-emotional learning to take place. These programs use the school's infrastructure to teach that a life free of violence and addiction is possible. They change habits that can lead to social ailments and create a stronger push toward academic excellence!

Enhance emotional education by providing enough counselors for your student population. Develop the counselors so that they can address bullying, maturity, anger management, and other issues that crop up in youth. Be aware of your community's demographics so that you can reduce the impact of poverty, incarceration, and other negative elements whenever students are at school.

THREAT MANAGEMENT

Threat management considers the emotional and psychological environment in which the people in your school interact. Managing threats, both actual and perceived, creates an atmosphere that is welcoming and warm. Your school becomes a place where learning occurs unobstructed.

Threat management requires observation and, where appropriate, action. The best tool any school has for managing threats is the atmosphere people encounter on campus. Your school should feel safe and inviting the moment an individual passes through the door. Classrooms should feel open and inclusive. Official spaces, like offices and meeting rooms, should convey the willingness of everyone involved with the school to listen, hear, and understand.

Many of the other recommendations in this book are building blocks for this atmosphere (for example, "Share Responsibilities," "Favorite Everyone!," and "Earn Respect"). Once you've set the tone, though, maintaining that tone comes from threat management. A proactive approach is a powerful way to ensure that threats to the atmosphere of well-being are dealt with before they become bigger issues for teachers or the student body.

Start with the details. Be aware of what microaggressions based on gender or racial identities look like. Train teachers to diffuse conflicts between students that happen inside the classroom as well as those that originate off campus. Encourage maintenance and security staff to watch for signs of emotionally troubled students. Since students tend not to have many interactions with this level of the staff, they might relax enough to signal that they're in trouble to the janitor or a cafeteria worker.

This kind of involvement is second nature to most people who choose a career in education, so you'll be tapping into your staff's baseline skillsets. You'll receive the full support of parents who want, most of all, for their children to be safe physically, emotionally, and psychologically.

FACE CONTROVERSY

Facing controversy turns some of your biggest challenges into opportunities to stay in front of issues.

Facing controversy enables rapid responses to issues that, if left unattended, might negatively impact your school. You'll prove that you're a true leader who's not afraid of a potential firestorm. You'll enhance the trust others have in you to lead the school.

At some point in their careers, all principals will be called on to face controversy. Debates crop up all the time in education! Evolution and intelligent design are still being fought over in courts, healthy initiatives in the cafeteria anger students, and the whole idea of charter schools can still be divisive. When you face controversy head on, you defend your students, teachers, and staff from the chaos. That's your job!

Face controversy with rapid and thoughtful responses. Consider the circumstances. Is it possible that a parent is upset about something else and is using this one thing as a weapon against the school? Are there broader social components over which your school has no control? Call on your trusted advisors to decide how to confront the controversy. Take steps to deal with the issue on an ongoing basis, and recognize that those steps might have to change as circumstances change. Once the controversy has passed, inform every one of the outcome to assure them that the school is still strong.

GO DIGITAL

Go digital to create operational efficiency and implement innovative ideas with minimal hassle using devices and apps your students already love.

Going digital harnesses the phones and tablets many students already own for education. It provides new ways to connect with students in a familiar format. By reducing the need for paper and other physical materials, going digital can even reduce your annual budget!

Schools across the nation are going digital. One way schools are getting around investing in expensive equipment is with Mouse Mischief by Microsoft. Students need only a mouse rather than a computer. The teacher integrates multiple-choice questions or other clickable components into presentations. When the teacher flips to a new picture or slide, students click on the answers they think are correct. In addition to reducing the school's budget and eliminating the complexity of laptops in the classroom, the program encourages interactive teaching that engages students.

Go digital using the free programs already available through shareware and apps. Sheppard Software's website offers registered versions of software programs to schools for free. Their selection includes geography games, test preparation courses, history and math software, and more. Use Twitter to set up microblogs where teachers can post reminders about tests or other events. Provide a forum where parents can connect with each other to create study groups, set up carpools, and reach out for help. Use Facebook's moderation tool to approve posts on a student page that enhances the community on campus.

DIG INTO DATA

Digging into data uncovers measurable information that will focus your efforts on opportunities to create real change.

Digging into data gives you a good understanding of the way things stand at your school. By tracking data over an academic year, you understand the progress of different initiatives. By year's end, you'll have another snapshot of how things stand. Compare the two to determine what worked, what needs a boost, and where to go next.

Dig into data to address tardiness and absenteeism. Rather than providing parents only with the not-so-welcome news about a child's attendance, you can present the issue as something that impacts the entire school. Late arrivals disrupt the flow of the day's lesson and interrupt other students' work. Absent children can't support others or generate new ideas for their class. With a bigger picture in hand, parents are that much more likely to implement proactive measures that get their kids to school on time.

Dig into data by reviewing incident reports, attendance sheets, disciplinary events, observations provided by teachers and counselors, and standardized test scores. Determine what's needed, such as better attendance or more staff development. Consider broad areas that need to be addressed like low grades or lack of parental involvement. Then dig deeper to determine whether the low grades are clustered in certain topical areas or whether parental involvement is being impacted by issues like the regional economy. With these details at hand, you are better prepared to implement change.

CONSTRUCTED CAREERS

Go beyond the annual career day by calling on small business owners and freelancers to share how students can create their own constructed careers.

Nowadays, families and individuals move much more often than they did a few decades ago. As people have become more mobile, the career opportunities available to them have also expanded. The American economy is driven in large part by small businesses and freelancing jobs. These careers tend to circulate income and intellectual property inside the community in which the individual lives and works, and are therefore a valuable part of the local economy. While some people think of freelancing or microbusinesses as side hustles, a great number of efforts that begin as supplementary jobs thrive and grow into businesses. Serve your students' futures by keying into constructed careers they can build themselves.

The digital natives sitting in your classrooms are primed and ready for constructed careers. So much of what can be done to generate income and build a business is accessible through a keyboard. Designing digital items like websites or apps, providing advice as a video blogger, offering freelance services, and much, much more can be performed online. The best part is that the students will tap into areas they're already familiar with to build their futures. As they work toward gathering more experience, they can connect with mentors and potential clients. You might even discover that more than a few of your students are already well on their way to turning their digital presence into an income stream.

Encourage students to take the next step by calling on small business owners and freelancers in your area. Ask them to visit classrooms or grade levels that make sense given their industry, or set up a symposium so that more students can attend. Ask visitors to focus on how they got their start, how they resolve their most common issues, and how they adapt to changing conditions. The talks don't have to be long. Do allow time for questions to be taken from the students, either live at the end or submitted in writing before the visitor arrives. You'll empower students to think about their futures in a new way. You'll give your community citizens who will build new opportunities for themselves and for others with constructed careers.

SMALL BITES

Small bites means break down each goal and task into individual steps.

Small bites help you tackle complex tasks and goals that seem overwhelming. It provides you with independent activities that can be scheduled and monitored. As the single units are completed, you'll be able to measure how quickly you're moving toward the final goal. This will enhance your motivation as well as that of your team!

Small bites can help you tackle new tasks and streamline older procedures. Before teacher evaluation time, consider how your school manages this task every year. Which staff members are involved? How is the information gathered? How are the evaluations created? When and where are they delivered? Then pull out your procedures manual and compare actual steps with those laid out in the procedures. You'll be surprised how many potential adjustments can make the process much less of a chore.

Approach each task with small bites in mind. Consider first the deadline. How many working days are available? Then consider who is going to complete the task. Write down the different components. If possible, assign individual steps to other people. Once they've completed their step, they can return to their regular duties; meanwhile, the burden on the primary movers has been reduced. Blend different steps together whenever it makes sense. By breaking the chore into small bites, you'll trim the schedule, reduce stress, and be able to measure progress at any point.

EXCELLENCE TRUMPS PERFECTION

Excellence trumps perfection keeps your focus on achievements and goals rather than the minor details that make something "less than perfect."

Excellence trumps perfection places real gains ahead of any concept of perfection. It prevents you from wasting time and resources on unattainable goals. Placing excellence above perfection allows students and staff the freedom to pursue goals in ways that suit them best.

Excellence trumps perfection when you're implementing federal and state regulations. Some of these will, of course, have to be followed to the letter. However, many provide enough flexibility that you can strive for excellence in implementation. Eliminate the hairsplitting and your school will move ahead faster and achieve more!

Remember that excellence trumps perfection when assessing your teachers as well as your own activities. With students, lifting failing academic performance into the passing or even average category is a demonstration of excellence. Administrative staff who demonstrate warmth and compassion toward parents and teachers provide excellence in their performance. If anyone doubts your approach, just point out that an A is still an A . . . even if one A was achieved by scoring a few points less than the other A!

EVENT SAFETY

A few creative, low-cost steps added to your existing event safety guidelines will allow your school to manage risk whenever it provides enriching programs.

Public events are loved by the students who participate, parents who attend, and the teachers and administrators who create the programs and bring them to life. When preparing plays, sports programs, afterschool activities, or other events where large numbers of people will gather, bolster your standard event safety procedures with steps tailored to your campus. Life can't be entirely risk-free, but with a little planning, you will make things much safer.

For any situation where the public is invited, prevention begins at the entrance. Ticketing all events, even those that are put on for free, creates a record of every individual who plans to attend. Ticketing also ensures that popular events don't become overcrowded. Position staff at key points inside the space where the event will take place. Give them a t-shirt or large badge so that visitors can identify them if they need help. Ensuring that they are immediately noticeable will also discourage individuals who might be inclined to spontaneously cause problems.

Control the space around the event by having volunteers patrol the halls or grounds around that building. Station helpers who are also visibly identified with large badges in the hallways through which attendees will travel to reach the restrooms. If needed, station volunteers at any doors beyond which attendees will not be allowed.

The National Center for Spectator Sports Safety and Security recommends that no one be allowed to reenter a facility once they've left. Consider implementing this simple measure to prevent individuals from bringing in contraband or using the event as an opportunity to snoop around other parts of campus. Have an evacuation plan in place in the event that weather, utility failure, or other issues require attendees to leave under unusual circumstances. And make sure that at least two individuals present have been trained in crowd supervision. This is as simple as knowing the signs that signal drug use, arguments, or other situations among attendees. When it comes to event safety, a little preparation goes a long way.

WISH LISTS

Wish lists allow individuals to talk about their needs, goals, and desires in a creative way.

Wish lists are supercharged suggestion boxes. They pinpoint needs that might otherwise go unnoticed or unfulfilled. They get people thinking about possibilities rather than probabilities, which can generate wonderful ideas. Wish lists also eliminate the expectations that might hover around a suggestion box. The whole idea of wishing is broad thinking about what could be rather than what "should" be!

Wish lists generate a mentality that is open creatively and free of expectations. It's an invitation for people to consider how they experience the school and what they would change if they could. The items on a wish list allow people to see not only what they want but how difficult it might be to reach those goals. The concept creates a powerful forum in which feedback, advice, ideas, and thoughts can be shared.

Generate wish lists for every area of your school. What wish lists will the administrative and support personnel create? Teachers can turn in wish lists related to their individual classrooms as well as the school. Students can provide wish lists about the curriculum, the library, after-school activities, or even the buses. Parental wish lists might address the property, how they interact with the school, or what they want for their students. When you fulfill items on wish lists, you become the principal who makes magic happen!

STUDENT ACTION COMMITTEES

Form a student action committee to generate change in your school as well as the larger community.

Student action committees offer a hands-on civic education to the young people at your school. Participation in the group will prepare them for a world that is constantly changing and always challenging.

Every initiative they undertake will hand them more tools with which to navigate the complex interconnections woven into modern social, political, and economic trends. In the safe setting of your campus, they can learn how to step out, support their own rights and the rights of others, and protect the free flow of ideas that move us all forward.

Recent events have brought a host of social issues to the table. When a student action committee selects one issue for its focus each year, the discussions and debates they'll engage in demand that they think deeply about the perspectives they formed before joining the group. The issue doesn't have to be political, although it might be; the area where they want to work might impact many people or only one group. The idea is to spur them to research all angles of a topic and then formulate steps that fit their stated mission.

The issues a student action committee might tackle range from economic inequality to the privatization of prisons, from child labor to discrimination in one of its many forms. Each topic requires that the group agree on which rights and responsibilities citizens currently hold, which rights and responsibilities citizens should hold, and how those rights and responsibilities might be secured for all. The action plan developed by the group should contain two parts. The first considers what they can do to support change; the second considers what institutions and governments can do to change society.

Students today are already concerned about a number of issues. When they join together to form a student action committee, they take control of their own futures. They develop a sense of agency that will fuel their current and future lives with power and purpose. And because their actions have a real potential to create long-lasting change, the sense of meaning they'll derive from their focused efforts will propel them to new heights in other areas.

Chapter 2

Wisdom for Your People

CHILDREN FIRST

Children first places students at the center of your academic universe. Put their needs at the top of your agenda . . . before teachers, parents, even yourself.

The wisdom of children first is simple: by placing students at the center of your universe, you automatically filter every action you take through the sieve of their needs. Every decision you make will resonate with their experiences in school as well as in their lives. Your approach will also signal to everyone around you that administrators, teachers, and staff are expected to follow.

Children first has been at the heart of public education since its inception. The first public school was founded in Boston in 1635. Free public schooling became available after the American Revolution revealed the importance of having a knowledgeable population. President John Adams said, "The whole people must take upon themselves the education of the whole people and be willing to bear the expenses of it." The students are the reason why you chose a profession in education. You are there to serve as their advocate.

Place children first with one easy step. When making decisions, always ask, *Is this good for children?* If the answer is *yes*, go for it. If the answer is *no*, don't do it.

INSPECT WHAT YOU EXPECT

Inspect what you expect provides quality control.

You are ultimately responsible for everything from the safety of the food served in the cafeteria to the number of accidents on campus. Inspecting what you expect from others ensures that every job is done right. It allows you to catch things that are wobbling before they jump off the track. It's part of being a good leader. Over the long run, your efforts will push your school to the forefront.

Inspecting what you expect isn't about micromanaging. Instead, it's about creating the best environment for learning. Inspecting what you expect identifies issues before they balloon out of control. The Wallace Foundation found that highly effective principals observe their school's operations frequently and provide immediate feedback on the basis of their observations. This approach supports teachers quickly and is more efficient because issues are never allowed to bloom into crises.

Inspecting what you expect is a constant process. Walking the long way to your office in the mornings and after lunch can reveal everything from student dynamics to maintenance issues. Sitting in on classrooms for a few minutes now and then—not just when there's a complaint—provides insight into the nuances of your teachers' performance. Chatting with parents before and after events can enhance your understanding of how their children experience your school. Inspect what you expect to ensure that every person performs at an exemplary level!

TAME TOXIC EMPLOYEES

Because your school is also a workplace, tame toxic employees to preserve morale and keep the focus on teaching and learning.

An overwhelming percentage of teachers and educators enter the profession in order to have a profound impact on young lives. Unfortunately, some of those same people can act in ways that seem better suited to a grade-school playground. Individuals who fulfill only the bare minimum requirements of their jobs, ones who complain constantly, and those who slip mildly negative comments into every conversation can turn your school into a very unpleasant place. To tame toxic employees, act early and decisively.

In human relationships, it's natural to write off problems. People can have difficult days when they don't present their best selves. As long as the issue isn't persistent, you're right to give your staff a break. But don't let a troublemaker continue indulging their negativity unfettered. Like water dripping on a stone, their attitude will erode the foundation you've worked so hard to build.

Approach toxic employees through the channels you've already built with them as professionals and as individuals. If you're new to the school and haven't had a chance to connect with this person, work on developing a baseline rapport. Once you've opened the door, tame the toxic employee by discussing the issue in a calm and controlled manner. Listen closely to their response. You might find that their dissatisfaction stems from a cause that's easily corrected. In other cases, their discontent will be based on something that either can't be changed or shouldn't be changed.

Use your own best self to guide them to better behavior. Compliment them on the things they do well. Let them know they are a valued part of the team, with an emphasis on "team." Acknowledge their difficulty accepting or resolving the issue. Point out the places where you also recognize that the problem is real. You'll honor their truth while building a common bridge. Then move into the resolution you'd like to see. Present your expectations in clear language and ask whether they need clarity on anything you've said. The rest of your school will thank you for taming toxic employees firmly and quickly.

NEVER TAKE SIDES

Never take sides means that, although you'll make judgments, you'll never judge.

Never taking sides is critical to every effective leader. Your teachers and staff need to know that their issues will be heard in a fair and safe environment. You'll utilize district rules as well as common sense to make your decisions, but you'll always be impartial. You'll never judge someone for past challenges or personal problems.

Never taking sides means that you'll implement the legal requirements while championing procedures that correct the flaws in those requirements. Never taking sides means that staffing decisions aren't popularity contests. Never taking sides means that people who work hard and have a passion for teaching control their own futures. Never taking sides means that people count—who they are, where they are, and what they want.

Never taking sides isn't always easy. It requires that you maintain a neutral, impartial, equitable, and objective viewpoint. When things heat up, nothing can be more difficult! Always be available. Always listen. Know that nothing outside of a true emergency ever has to be decided in the moment. You can always take a day, an hour, or a few minutes to step aside, reflect calmly, and then render your decision from a foundation of strength that stems from fairness.

SELF-HARM

Monitor the school's population for evidence of self-harm to rapidly address issues that prevent students from becoming whole, healthy learners.

Self-harm does not include actions associated with suicidal ideations. Instead, this type of activity creates wounds or injuries that are deliberately self-inflicted. The act of self-harm is intended to distract the individual from emotions that are unpleasant or overwhelming, to use pain to counteract a feeling of being numb to life, to exert control when feeling helpless or out of control, or to punish themselves for some perceived wrong.

Although cutting and burning can be obvious, a student might also stick themselves with pins, scratch their skin, or hit themselves. Covering wounds or undertaking activities that leave less obvious wounds can fool adults into thinking that nothing is going on. Every person in the school, from maintenance staff up to the administrators, should be taught to recognize the signs. Students who wear long sleeves or pants in hot weather or under uniforms, those who suffer from frequent "accidents," and those who keep a supply of sharp objects or lighters on hand should be monitored for evidence of self-harm.

When developing a protocol to address this issue in your population, start with the suicide prevention protocols you already have in place. Utilize the areas where they overlap, such as referring suspected cases to the crisis team. From there, determine the steps to take to address the behaviors. Start with broad questions that reference the student's demeanor, and ask whether there are issues they want help with. If needed, move into specific questions that call out specific signs like old scars or covering up their arms. From there, teachers can guide individuals to the nurse and the counselor for help.

You'll also need to determine when parents will be notified of the behaviors. Maintain a list of external resources for when you need to refer families for assistance, and for those times when things progress beyond the school's ability to intervene. Since copying self-harm behaviors, particularly self-cutting, is seen at higher rates among girls, assure any student who reports a potential issue with another student that they've done the right thing for their friend. With careful steps and compassionate attitudes, you'll help the students who self-harm as well as those who might copy their actions.

INSPIRE TO ASPIRE

The Latin root of inspire and aspire translates as "breathe" or "breathe life into." When you inspire to aspire, you breathe life into your staff and your school. You inspire your teachers to aspire for more; they inspire their students to aspire for even higher levels.

Inspiring to aspire recognizes excellence and supports passion. When successful teachers are recognized, they become resources other teachers can turn to. When teachers become leaders, they inspire their peers to reach higher. And since passion in the classroom spurs student growth, inspiring to aspire impacts your entire school.

Inspiring to aspire isn't found in the school where some teachers stand above their colleagues. Instead, it's found in places where teachers stand beside their peers. Inspiring to aspire emphasizes collegiality rather than a hierarchy. Sean McComb, 2014's National Teacher of the Year, stated that human capital is outstripped by social capital. When teachers support each other, they inspire each other to aspire. Trust increases, candor spreads, and everyone takes responsibility for everyone's success.

Inspiring to aspire takes many forms. Set up an in-school blog where anyone can post thoughts and share anecdotes from their classrooms. Encourage an informal system of mentorship, or formalize the system by assigning new hires to a more accomplished guide. Encourage individuals who are undertaking research to share their discoveries at voluntary monthly meetings. Inspire to aspire throughout your school!

SHARE YOUR VISION

Sharing your vision looks beyond today. You know the goals you've set for the students, the school, and everyone who works there. Share that vision of tomorrow!

Sharing your vision proves to teachers and parents that their leader is reaching for results today and in the future. Sharing that picture proves that every step is taken for the greater good. When the image of the future is bright, short-term challenges are met with more vigorous efforts. By lifting the entire school, all individuals connected with the school benefit. Prove that their trust is well placed by sharing your vision.

Sharing your vision resonates with the aspirations and goals of teachers, students, and parents. We all want the best education, the best options, and the best results. Sharing your vision allows others to see around the obstacles and recognize that there is a way forward. A singular vision allows support to coalesce around one goal. People from many different areas pull together to build a road to that future.

Sharing your vision should be implemented in several steps. Set out your long-term goal as a broad image. You might be reaching for true inclusion in a diverse district or a higher national rank. Describe what the school will look like on a day-to-day basis when that goal has been reached. Then break that vision down into steps. Lay out the things that need to happen in three years, in one year, in six months. Show how each step will provide immediate benefits that will result in your vision coming to life.

LISTEN

When you truly listen to someone, you do more than hear their words. You provide them with your full attention. You register not just what their words say but also what their body language tells you.

The ability to listen is a wise trait. When people know their leader listens, they work harder. They perform at a higher level and feel secure in their positions. They trust that although you might not have all the answers right away, you'll consider their issues and search for solutions. Listening shows that you care . . . about the school, the students, and the individuals who are the backbone of the educational process.

When you listen, you take actions on the basis of what you've heard. The teacher with a new idea is allowed to implement unique techniques. The maintenance staff is allocated the resources they need. Students believe wholeheartedly that they have an advocate in a position of authority. Actions that flow from listening impact the issue at hand and enhance the trust required for long-term effectiveness.

Make time to listen. Some people will feel heard during a quick chat in a busy hallway. Others will prefer to schedule a private conversation. Recognize how the speaker's prior experiences might impact their perspective and display empathy. Convey your engagement with a nod, a smile, or a hand gesture. And since most people comprehend only about 25 percent of what they hear, always be willing to ask questions or return to the issue with that person later.

CELEBRATE WITH STAFF

Coordinate with your leadership team to identify areas where you can celebrate with staff on a monthly basis. These special, ongoing events will support educators and enhance retention numbers.

This idea is all about building a sense of community and connection among the people who work on your campus. We are all more than our careers. When you find areas and activities to celebrate with staff, you focus on the interests and passions that make them well-rounded human beings. Inviting workers to bring their full selves to school creates an atmosphere in which real connections can be formed. When people feel that their best selves are welcome on campus, they bring their best selves to their classrooms.

Divide the areas you celebrate with staff into those with local ties and those with broader appeal. Locally, you might key in on state sports teams, natural wonders found only in your region, or historic events that generate a sense of civic pride. Add in ones with broader appeal like clothing fashions popular in previous decades, characters from meaningful novels, or a movie that highlights an important moment or issue. Assign each topic to a different month of the academic year. Be sure to pick days that won't interfere with other school events.

The celebrations can take different forms every month. For example, Old-school Dress Day might encourage staff to arrive at school wearing an outfit that was popular during the decade they attended high school. Movie Day can provide a showing of a specific film in the lounge after classes end. The Sports Day celebration can festoon the break room with the team's logo while encouraging staff to wear the team's colors. The topics can change year to year for variety or to accommodate interests your people want to celebrate.

When setting up days to celebrate with staff, don't overreach. Keep the ideas focused on fun and relaxing premises. This isn't a work assignment for anyone; it's a chance to feel free sharing lifelong passions and small pleasures. When your staff has access to a consistent, recurring channel through which to exchange personal experiences, they'll bond in new ways. And that definitely deserves to be celebrated.

SHARE YOUR KNOWLEDGE

Sharing knowledge allows individuals to create new knowledge.

When you share your knowledge, you discover new ways to enhance the learning process. New skills are learned, teachers are integrated across disciplinary categories, and unique ideas are sparked. This process has long been accepted in the corporate world because it generates a competitive edge. Implement the same process to lift your school's rank and enhance the educational experience.

Sharing knowledge happens all the time. When teachers chat about their techniques, they provide other teachers with new ideas. When principals share their knowledge about state and national standards, teachers ensure that students meet those standards. When principals share their planning skills, teachers connect students to the curriculum more efficiently.

Share your knowledge on a regular basis. You might send out a weekly e-mail with a short anecdote about something you've encountered and what resulted from that encounter. At least half of these anecdotes should be positive stories that highlight what's good about your school and staff. Every month, distribute a list of upcoming development opportunities. Openly share during meetings and informal encounters. Your openness will encourage openness among teachers, creating a dynamic and passionate atmosphere. Shared knowledge is truly one of a school's greatest resources!

RESPECT OTHERS

In school and in life, many types of respect can be offered to others. For principals who have to deal with people from every walk of life, only one type matters: respect for others' feelings.

Respecting others makes your job easier. By respecting the feelings, thoughts, and opinions of parents, teachers, and students, you'll connect with them more quickly. Communication flows easily, others recognize how much you care, and trust becomes your foundation.

Respect runs deeper than basic courtesy. It's about probing for the real reason a parent might be concerned about a certain policy. It's about discovering why a teacher might resist new procedures. It's about elevating students who might be neglected by adults at home so they realize that they count. Respecting others means that no matter who they are or where they've come from, people will be treated equally.

Offer respect by looking people in the eye. Schedule your engagements so that teachers receive the time they need from you. Provide the same courtesy to students that adults demand from them. Always respond to e-mails, if only to alert the sender that you need more time to reply fully. Have an assistant return calls that need to be scheduled. Keep your promises, even small ones, to convey how much you respect others.

COMMUNICATE

Communicate means to convey your message in a clear and inspirational way, to touch on the passion in your teachers to teach and in your students to learn.

Communicating provides important information your staff and students need to know. It also conveys your excitement over new initiatives and allows others to be excited about the future. Communication that resonates with listeners allows you to reach further and achieve more than bland directives.

Communicating takes place every time you interact with others. A quick chat with a teacher in the hall, speaking at a parents' meeting, and school-wide e-mails are the most common examples. You also communicate with your body language and word choices. A truly pleased smile, posture that is alert and attentive, and an open hand that invites participation are all effective forms of communication.

Communicate by saying what you mean. Don't sugarcoat bad news, and you'll communicate both information and your trust that others can handle the news. Communicate through dialogues that encourage others to contribute. Keep it simple and, when asked or when necessary, follow up with the more complex point in the moment and later in writing. Focus on the big issues or ideas even when conveying small details. Know who you're talking to . . . and adapt your words accordingly.

BLENDED LEARNING

A school's ability to offer blended learning, a process by which students are provided with both distance and in-person lessons, has become more important since the pandemic. Having protocols in place will address future interruptions to in-person education. Blended learning also enhances accessibility for students who find it difficult to attend in person.

Blended learning ensures that every student benefits by learning from educators within a group of their peers. With distance learning, the most effective approach uses class time to introduce new concepts and information. Students then explore the topic further on their own, or they work on their own to apply the new ideas by completing assignments. Then, when class resumes (either online or in person), individuals present their conclusions and solutions to the group.

If you already allow digital devices in the classroom, you'll be ahead of the game for blended learning. The same apps and feeds students already use will integrate seamlessly into distance learning. When you lay out your blended learning plan, address delivery methods, meeting software, and other technical details, including ways teachers can observe learners while they work online. Define the level of personal interaction that should occur between teachers and students. Also set a minimum number of interactive activities students should complete during the year. Opportunities for feedback and reflection will ensure that distance learning is as powerful as in-person efforts.

A key element for long-term success is to teach students how to manage themselves. Offer examples of how to schedule study time, set goals, and self-evaluate progress to build a strong foundation. Teachers might even have individuals predict their test scores as a way to focus effort and bolster academic results. Provide checklists that break down each task into different milestones to students and their parents. Have teachers monitor the progress of the checklists and assess students as they move forward. Give students the option to share their work through online uploads, and have them review the work of others. Peer support will encourage individuals to complete assignments and spur them to exceed their own expectations.

FAVORITE EVERYONE!

Favoriting everyone is a twist on not playing favorites. Instead of singling out a few individuals for special treatment, treat everyone as special!

When you favorite everyone, you demonstrate that you expect their best in every moment. Your expectations prove that they are important and unique, and that you're open to everything they can offer. Students will aspire to achieve more and teachers will know that they are valued and trusted. Favoriting everyone creates a school that works together because each individual values others for who they are. Favoriting everyone spreads goodwill, enhances dedication, and creates loyalty.

Favoriting everyone happens when you set standards. Student behavior, test scores, national rankings, and school procedures should be achievable . . . and high. Day by day, favorite students by commenting on individual efforts and accomplishments. Favorite your teachers by recognizing different departments throughout the academic year. Favorite parents by inviting them to a year-end lunch with teachers and students in the cafeteria. Broadcasting these expectations creates pride as individuals work toward those goals.

One of the simplest and most effective ways to favorite everyone is through positive feedback. Complimenting students on how well they've followed the dress code proves that the school's rules are neither arbitrary nor thoughtless. Publicizing the newest teaching initiative or rise in test scores in the parents' newsletter emphasizes that the leader respects the teachers' efforts. Clean bathrooms, stringent food-safety procedures, and neatly landscaped grounds should all be pointed out as achievements.

PROACTIVE INCLUSION

Proactive inclusion invites people from every background into your school.

Proactive inclusion allows everyone at your school to participate and be heard, no matter what their background or status is. A school is only as strong as its individual members. By integrating every one of those individuals, your school adapts quickly to changing circumstances. Proactive inclusion ensures that every student and teacher is given the full resources they need to succeed. That propels the success of you, your students, and the entire school!

Proactive inclusion is as varied a process as the individuals you work with. Nowhere is the impact seen more clearly than in decision-making. A group consensus by its very nature requires that all voices be allowed to speak. As different elements are championed, individuals learn about the benefits of each option. Eventually the group determines the best path forward, given the current circumstances. When the group makes a decision, the group buys into the efforts their decision requires. They become champions for the end goal and tirelessly strive to achieve that goal.

Proactive inclusion is about managing individuals. When you notice that one teacher hasn't offered any comments during a meeting, draw them out with questions. Individuals who overpower other voices should be gently deflected. Parents can be encouraged to provide ideas and comments by e-mail and students can cast their votes on issues that involve something with which they can help. When all voices sing together, the result is harmonious.

CELEBRATE WITH STUDENTS

Connect with student leaders to draw up a list of events tied to curricular topics you can celebrate with students.

Celebrating with students puts a fun spin on learning and education. By focusing on educational subjects in a new way, learners engage with unique elements related to standard topics like science and math. Because the celebrations reach beyond the textbooks for inspiration, these activities can support racial and cultural identities, spur an interest in historical figures, and encourage today's youth to reach for the best in their future.

All these benefits derive from the fairly simple concept of celebrating with students on a recurring basis. Ideally, you'll be able to plan one of these events for every month of the academic year. History and science curriculums are bursting with discoveries, people, and events that can become focal points. Select topics from less traditional learning areas like arts and culture, as well. The mix will achieve the greatest level of engagement and reach the widest number of students.

Be as creative with the celebrations as your school can allow. For Math Day, students can be asked to come dressed as their favorite mathematician. Girls might show up as Ada Lovelace, while Latino students might don their best Jaime Escalante or Ruth Gonzalez impersonation. Science Day can offer a lobby display filled with everyday items that come from scientific developments, like shampoo and baby powder. In a different year, the display can hold items that demonstrate basic scientific principles (a cooking pan for heat transference in physics; a bottle of vitamins for the applied science involved in healthcare).

When the arts are selected as the topic to celebrate with students, your opportunities for creative implementation are endless. The event could be broadly based on a single art form like music, or it could be specific to a certain type of musical performance such as singing. A celebration of music could collect a "mixed tape" recording of the first bar from every song submitted by the student population. During a celebration of collage, students can build a collage by taping scraps of fabric or paper cutouts onto the floor.

Whenever you celebrate with students, be sure to record the activity with photos or videos. The moments you capture will make great additions to your social media and newsletters. Sharing the highlights will present your school's exciting approach to learning and education. You'll encourage students to discover new things on their own while acknowledging their efforts in public. Considering how creative young people can be, your school and the school community are bound to enjoy every event.

REFLECTIVE LEADERSHIP

Reflective leadership is a method that allows you to access situations and make decisions with a new perspective.

Reflective leadership is all about awareness. It allows you to communicate effectively by focusing on the message you want to send. By its very nature, it requires you to assess your own strengths and weaknesses in specific situations. You can then assess the strengths and weaknesses of others to locate the best person to tackle the issue.

Reflective leadership reaches its true heights in a school setting. Schools thrum with the beautiful chaos created when individuals of every age and from every background join together for a common purpose. To create true cohesion, the leader must know what individuals can give others. Reflective principals know themselves well and apply the same assessments to others. By knowing others well, the reflective leader builds a thriving environment.

Integrate reflective leadership with a few steps. Identify a challenge or a situation that needs to be addressed. Step back and study the issue from an outsider's perspective. Ultimately this will lead you to frame the challenge in a proper context. Then consider how you and individuals in your network have addressed similar conditions in the past. Select the approaches that have worked and begin testing them to find the best solution. This reflective process becomes more natural the more you use it, allowing you to resolve issues more quickly and assess situations with greater accuracy.

LOVE YOUR PEOPLE

Loving your people is a directive to praise in public and discipline in private.

Loving your people allows you to nurture the best of who people are and to help them move beyond their limits. When you praise in public, you validate an individual's efforts with your attention and the attention of others. By disciplining in private, you preserve an individual's relationships with coworkers and peers. Loving your people means you respect them for more than their work . . . you respect them as part of the school's culture.

Loving your people is important for students and teachers. When students receive awards or are complimented in front of their peers, they become role models. Students who require disciplinary actions should be sheltered from the harassment that might result if other students are privy to the corrective measures. Teachers who are promoted, given awards, or otherwise recognized publicly become role models; they also send the message to students and parents that the school cares about quality. Disciplinary actions should always be conducted in private settings to eliminate shame.

Love your people by broadcasting rewards, honors, and other validation. Pop your head into the gym and cheer a random class. Personally congratulate every student who runs for student council . . . even if they don't win. Send a quick e-mail to teachers who lead afterschool programs to thank them for their effort. Send an ecard thanking every parent who volunteers. Loving your people is an easy step that imbues your school with positive, supportive energy!

EMOTIONAL SUPPORT

Ensuring that everyone at your school receives emotional support is a key element to creating a safe environment for teaching and learning.

Emotional support is sometimes considered to be a task for student counselors. However, meaningful support is provided by every individual in a school, and it is provided for every individual on campus. Staff must be given the time they need to listen deeply to individuals who reach out. Acknowledging a young person's discomfort, even over issues that might appear small to an adult, makes them feel heard. Rather than launching immediately into a solution, asking questions about what the student can do to address the issue gives them the power to take charge.

Teachers and staff also need emotional support. Regularly send out tips and ideas for managing stress. Encourage self-care by providing lists of external resources. Encourage your people to cultivate strong relationships during their daily encounters with others who work on campus. One of the best ways to enhance the connections between individuals is to organize social activities scheduled outside of school hours. These gestures will reduce burnout and improve retention rates. Your school will benefit immediately.

As always, effective ideas can be budget friendly. Consider setting aside a "quiet room" where anyone can pop in for ten minutes to recharge. Keep the overhead lights off and use desk lamps aimed at the walls to generate a soothing atmosphere. Ban the use of cell phones or any devices that generate sound in the space. Unless conversations are required to calm a particularly upset individual, chatting should be discouraged. Provide basic drawing supplies, even if it's just a whiteboard, for therapeutic doodling. With a mini-retreat easily available, you'll be surprised at how quickly students and teachers can tame their problems and return to the classroom with a refreshed attitude.

ENCOURAGE COLLABORATION

Encourage collaboration among teachers and between students to enhance educational performance.

Encouraging collaboration among teachers is a key way to improve student achievement levels. Teachers learn from each other when they collaborate; and by extension, their students learn more easily. Collaboration allows people to share strategies, offer anecdotes from their own experiences, and benefit from the wisdom of others.

Encouraging collaboration can have surprising results. Aspire Public Schools, a nonprofit charter, was ranked as 2011's Most Improved School in an international report after implementing joint lesson planning. Sparks Middle School in La Puente, California, implemented a variety of collaborative efforts yet spent roughly half per student as a similar middle school in its district. Encourage collaboration for a low-cost, high-impact effect!

Encourage collaboration by providing space and time for teachers to meet and exchange notes. Ask teachers who work with similar grade levels and subjects to get together. Encourage them to share challenges with students who are struggling to discover how other students have been guided to success. During these meetings, have teachers demonstrate lesson plans, create curriculum-based games, and schedule visits to each other's classes every month.

BE FRIENDLY, NOT FRIENDS

Be friendly, not friends means you maintain employer-employee relationships with teachers and staff and leader-follower relationships with parents and students.

Be friendly, not friends helps you focus on what's most important. When you treat people in a friendly manner, you strengthen your relationships. Friendship doesn't help you meet goals or get things done. Friendliness, however, makes people comfortable enough to work at their maximum abilities. And by understanding that friendly doesn't equal friendship; you won't feel disappointed when individuals don't support your every cause.

Be friendly, not friends eliminates the complications of the friend/employer scenario. If you're friends with staff or students, the extra attention might be mistaken for favoritism. Others will be less likely to respect your authority, weakening your ability to do what's best for the school. Individuals who reveal personal issues might turn to you during school hours, and you might share personal information that isn't appropriate for staff or others to know. Being friendly, not friends keeps your relationships professional and the operations smooth.

The best way to be friendly, not friends is to define your boundaries. Recognize when someone is growing attached and direct them to someone who is a more appropriate recipient of their attention . . . usually someone in their peer group. Recognize when your natural affinity with an individual might be moving into more intimate territory and remove yourself from situations where you might overshare. Boundaries make interactions simple for you and for everyone who interacts with you. And that's just plain productive!

BEFORE THE AFTER

Offer elective before the after classes or programs to prepare students for life after graduation.

The concepts and information involved in before the after set your students up for success. High school is a busy and stressful time for most young people. Providing them with specific advice about the steps they should take to prepare for their adult lives will help relieve some of that stress. When they do graduate, you'll release a flock of capable citizens into your community and into college. Your guidance will serve them now and in the future.

Often, schools that offer before the after assistance work primarily with seniors and perhaps with juniors. To garner the best results from your program, implement different levels of advice and assistance for each of the four high school grades. Start in freshman year by providing the time and equipment students need to conduct research related to possible career choices. Cultivate good study habits by providing short presentations on time management, organization of class materials, and how to listen and take effective notes.

The following year, provide sophomores with the resources they need to apply for honors and AP classes. Introduce good workplace habits by having teachers pretend to be employers while students play out the role of employee. This role-playing will enhance their ability to integrate into teams and give them effective communication experience. Provide information about colleges and career fairs, and consider whether you can arrange for sophomores to attend fairs in person or tour colleges virtually. Let the students discuss their experiences visiting fairs and talking with employers so that others can learn from them.

In junior year, encourage students to visit the colleges they're considering. Help them research ways to pay for higher education. Point them toward state and federal grants, and encourage research into private funding sources that focus on specific demographics. Seniors can take college and career certification tests, submit college and internship applications, fill out scholarship forms, and gather letters of recommendation from their teachers. Use the before the after program to keep their eyes on the prize that comes from higher education and a satisfying career. Every year, you'll launch a class of winners.

PROMOTE PARENTS

Promoting parents means encouraging parental participation at a multitude of levels.

Promoting parents enhances the entire educational process. No matter what a child's background, their parents' involvement results in higher grades, better test scores, steadier attendance, easier matriculation to the next grade level, and higher graduation and postsecondary education rates. Promoting parents also enhances students' social skills, improves their behavior, and motivates them to achieve more.

The Southwest Educational Development Laboratory found that promoting parents prompts children "to do better in school, stay in school longer, and like school more." Since school-age children spend 70 percent of their time outside school, parental involvement is important to the educational process. In fact, one of the most consistent predictors of academic achievement is a parent's expectation of educational success.

Promote parents early and often. Encourage students to practice reading at home with their parents. Alert parents to television programs that relate to the curriculum before a class tackles the subject. Set up a resource page on the school's website with links to local destinations that tie into lessons. When you point out that these activities also enhance the parent-child bond, you might find parents becoming much more active in their children's education!

PEOPLE SUCCEED

People succeeding refocuses all the attention paid to test scores, school rankings, and other statistics to what really counts: the students, teachers, and parents who make up your school.

Remembering that schools don't succeed, people succeed, puts the focus back where it belongs. Students who enter a school that is focused on their education and well-being are inspired to aspire, become lifelong learners, and contribute to their communities as adults. Teachers hired by a school focused on their success arrive early to innovative techniques, assist their peers, and invite parents into the educational process. Parents who interact with people-focused schools respect the principal, align their goals with the school's goals, and participate more.

People succeed when schools recognize the value of the human element. Rather than being an organization that doles out lessons, the school becomes a group of individuals who have joined together to encourage, inspire, and educate the community's children. They become their own community of like-minded individuals from various backgrounds and are linked by a common goal.

Allow people to succeed in your school. Always put the student first. Align all goals toward the educational, social, and psychological needs of the student body. Rally teachers by connecting with them on a human level, offering support, and creating an atmosphere in which respect is mutual. Include parents through frequent updates, message boards, and informal meet-and-greet opportunities. When your people succeed, your school automatically succeeds!

RACIAL AND ETHNIC IDENTITY

Support racial and ethnic identities through the school's culture as well as its physical environment.

Racial and ethnic identities have always been important, and schools that actively support the continuation and expression of those identities foster a dynamic, creative, and inclusive atmosphere. A physical environment that reflects how highly a person's identity is valued sends a clear message. Display artwork inspired by traditions found in different cultures. Pull together displays that highlight the histories of the different identities represented in your student body. Translate your school's motto into various languages, print the different versions on banners, and hang them throughout the school.

Once students enter the classroom, they should find active ways to support their racial and ethnic identities. Encourage teachers to integrate multicultural elements into their curriculum. Allow students to experiment with cultural competence by discussing how different societies solve everyday problems. Reach out to schools in other countries to set up "sister classes" students can interact with via letters, e-mails, videos, and podcasts. Ask for volunteers among educators and staff to share stories about growing up with their own identities.

Parents will often respond positively to these efforts, so be sure to pull them in as resources. Seek out volunteers who will give talks about what the various holidays celebrated in their cultures mean to their families. Organize an annual cultural festival featuring displays students have created to represent different traditions and norms. Pull together a cookbook using traditional recipes sent in by parents and grandparents.

Use social media to widen the impact beyond your campus. Ask students to write posts or even blog entries about their cultures. Encourage individuals to write up descriptions of the various events they participate in, highlighting why it's important to their identities. Ask for photos of traditional clothing or objects that have special meanings. Your students will be fostering understanding in your school and beyond. The community will recognize your school as a place that welcomes everyone.

STUDENTS ARE SPECIAL

Students are special means that you treat every student as if they were the only student.

Students are special is your school's key to academic success. When every child feels wanted and supported by the person in charge, they try harder. They feel a greater pull to attend and to show up on time. Test scores rise and your school ranks higher. Most important of all, you create an environment that is nurturing and emotionally safe.

Students are special all the time. A Civic Enterprises study for the Bill and Melinda Gates Foundation looked at the top five reasons students fail to complete school. Over 40 percent spent time with others who weren't interested in education, while 38 percent lacked rules that encouraged academic achievement. Yet 81 percent said graduating was important! When asked about how they would do things differently, 74 percent were committed to staying in school. When everything else in a student's life doesn't support education, the input of a caring, involved principal can make the difference.

Demonstrate that students are special in meaningful ways. Don't speak to kids only when they've done something wrong. Every time you walk the halls, interact with them with a friendly nod or a wave. Make an effort to have your first interaction with every child feel positive. By the time a student appears in your office because of disruptive behavior, you should already have connected with him or her on a different level. Stand at the end of the lunch line now and then to pass out milk or napkins. Stop into every classroom one day a week. Thirty seconds is enough! Just be there at different times and in different ways to prove how special they are to you.

BEWARE BELIEFS

Beware beliefs helps you recognize the false beliefs individuals hold and move beyond them to a productive interaction.

Beware beliefs helps you pinpoint the false "knowledge" students, parents, and staff might bring into your school. By recognizing that past experiences can weaken current efforts, you are better able to pull everyone together to meet your school's common goals. Cooperation increases, group identity grows stronger, and educational achievement is better served.

Beware beliefs that are detrimental to your school. The previous year's academic performance, challenges, and issues can snarl today's efforts even if those issues were resolved. A great example is found in bullying. Even if your school has avoided any major incidents, the prevalence of bullying among youth can worry parents, students, and teachers. Be clear about your antibullying policies and showcase the efforts that prevent bullying in your school. Beware the belief that bullying is unavoidable to keep it from taking over the educational process.

Beware beliefs by being aware of beliefs. Listen closely to what parents or staff tell you. When they speak of an issue, are they demonstrating a lot of emotional turmoil? Do they provide details that seem unrelated to the issue? These types of flags usually indicate that a belief is preventing them from seeing the situation clearly. Explore those beliefs with them or ask a peer they trust to sit in on your conversations to encourage exploration. Once you discover the belief, you can change the belief by providing evidence about how the situation really stands.

HELP THE HOMELESS

Help the homeless students in your school by providing a safe, nurturing environment that sets them up for success despite the very real difficulties they face.

Schools might not think about becoming involved with homelessness until they discover that a student is living in a shelter or a motel. Often, young people without a home are embarrassed by their situation and aren't eager to reveal details to their teachers or even their peers. Keep an eye out for signs like difficulty staying awake during class, lack of some or most of the documents needed for enrollment, poor hygiene, and unexplained absences. You or a trusted teacher can take students you're worried about aside for a private talk and offer to help the homeless.

Once you've confirmed that a student is homeless, take steps to help meet their basic needs. Ensure that they have access to nutritional food by directing their parents to food banks, and enroll the child in the lunch program. Connect them with individuals who can help them get into a safe shelter, and round up donations of clothing appropriate for the local weather. Arrange for them to shower in the gym facilities. Ask local charity thrift shops to provide vouchers for household items. Reassure the student that, by working together, they can stay on an academic pathway.

After basic needs are met, move on to other areas where the school can help the homeless. Be sure to assess the student's actual educational level rather than assuming they've been enrolled in the proper grade. See if they could benefit from tutoring by teachers or peers. Provide a quiet place where these young people can go after school to complete their homework assignments. Look into how government programs or grants offered by nonprofits can fund their college educations. Connect with local work experience programs so they can learn the skills they'll need when they enter the workforce.

Your efforts will have a huge impact on the child's mental health and well-being. School will become a place of stability and security in their lives. On campus, they'll receive the emotional support every young person craves, and they'll feel more integrated with their peer group. The attention you provide will comfort kids who might get lost in a family's constant rush to deal with crises. Help for the homeless offers the experience of success that might otherwise be lacking in a student's life. They'll learn that they are capable of dealing with difficult situations and will head into their own lives fully prepared.

STRENGTHEN WEAK LINKS

Strengthening weak links is about shoring up areas that might cause trouble among students or staff, or in the operation of your school.

Strengthening weak links allows you to manage people without judgment. When you help a teacher perform better, you prove that he or she can be valuable to the school. Guiding students to better performance or behaviors provides them with self-confidence because they realize they are important to someone in authority. Strengthening weak links makes your entire school stronger!

Strengthening weak links applies to policies as much as people. Teacher evaluations that are poorly received might indicate that the feedback isn't resonating properly. Something as simple as a change in format can help. Rather than provide only checklists or numerical rankings, consider adding a narrative that lays out strengths and areas that need improvement. If a narrative is already provided, consider whether less formal language will soften the blow in improvement requests or whether it might convey positive comments more directly. Policies impact people, so strengthening weak policies will strengthen your people!

Strengthen weak links by emphasizing compassion and awareness. Recognize that the weakness is usually already known by the individual. Approach them with the attitude that they are valuable and convey compassion for extenuating circumstances that might cause the weakness. You might not be able to address any of the external pressures, but a sympathetic ear can go a long way. When you strengthen weak links, everyone in your school knows that their own weaknesses will be treated with fairness and compassion.

WORK THE ROOM

Working the room means using every available asset—primarily people—to meet your school's goals.

Working the room is beneficial in two huge ways. First, it allows you to utilize the individual talents and abilities of everyone associated with your school regardless of age or background. The blend of individuals you assemble for a specific task will ensure the diversity and breadth necessary to succeed . . . and even to overachieve! Second, every individual at your school has an entirely different set of people they know. Whenever you tap into a student, parent, or staff member, you can reach through them to individuals far beyond the academic arena.

Working the room enhances the impact of fundraising efforts. Fundraisers are perfect opportunities to ask individuals who can't offer financial assistance to reach out to their network for donations. Whether they do that or not, you can ask for their help with that project or a different project. Even when individuals can't help, they might connect with someone who can.

Work the room with a single step: ask. Ask for help. Ask for feedback. Ask for time, experience, and other people's wisdom. Ask them into the school in a dozen ways. Ask them to reach out to others who might donate time, experience, or wisdom. Ask and your school shall receive!

TEACHER SHORTAGES

Prevent or address teacher shortages to protect educational opportunities and outcomes, especially among students with the greatest needs.

Although various efforts address teacher shortages at the state and local levels, principals have a significant impact on attracting educators and retaining the best teachers. The leadership qualities that make a principal effective are often the same ones teachers consider when weighing a decision to stay or leave. Assuming that life events or new careers are not part of the mix, dedicated educators tend to stay with principals who express their high regard for their people.

The easiest way to prevent teacher shortages is, of course, to ensure that individuals are happy with their current positions. Leaders who tell their teachers, both in person and in group situations, that their presence is valued inspire loyalty. When working with individuals who do decide to leave, clearly communicate that they will be welcomed back if they decide that the new position isn't for them. Never hesitate to follow up with star teachers a few months after they leave to let them know that the door is still open. Sometimes individuals regret their decision but can't bring themselves to say it out loud. Help them start the journey back, and your students will win.

Create an atmosphere that reduces the frequency with which people consider leaving. Check in with your educators throughout the school year to ask how things are going. Let them alert you to issues that might not be on your radar. Follow up for more details, and always ask for their ideas on how to resolve the challenge. When teachers tell you about things that are going well, follow up on those comments, too. Give credit to the people and programs that made those good things happen, and assure educators that those benefits will continue to roll in.

Finally, publicly recognize the impact your teachers have on students and parents. Call out top performance in staff messages. Follow up after tough periods with thanks that come directly from you. The more contact you have with your teachers, the more they'll want to stay in a place where they are important enough to garner your attention.

FOSTER ARTISTS

Fostering artists nurtures individuals who achieve in regular, reliable ways . . . like artists who work in relative obscurity every day.

Fostering artists ensures that the majority of your people aren't left behind or ignored. Since most teachers and students will perform in the middle range, they are the workhorses of your school. Supporting their achievements ensures that they don't feel lost when attention goes mostly to poor performers and top stars.

Foster artists to motivate and enhance the performance of 60 percent of your people. When principals focus too much on the tails—the top and bottom performers—they risk alienating the middle majority who perform reliably and consistently. When you attend to the middle, you might enhance individual achievement by small amounts. But the cumulative impact of many individuals making small gains boosts your school's overall performance a lot!

Foster artists with programs specifically aimed at improving their skills and rewarding their efforts. Every time you announce a top-performing student's accomplishments, recognize someone from the middle. Whenever a teacher excels beyond expectations, herald the accomplishments of a peer who improved on the basis of where they started. Fostering just a few of your artists tells the rest that their efforts are recognized and respected!

RECOGNIZE GOOD BEHAVIOR

Recognizing good behavior provides ongoing support to your students and staff.

Recognize good behavior to bolster the environment you want at your school. When people are recognized as good school citizens, the campus becomes safe and stable. Individuals know they are being recognized for conducting themselves in appropriate ways. Others know they are safe from bullying, violence, and the negative effects of rules that have been disregarded.

Recognizing good behavior is especially important for students who don't act out and teachers who perform well. When they are recognized for consistently good behavior, those behaviors are validated and their efforts continue as before. For individuals with behavioral issues, recognizing the smallest good behavior provides them with supportive feedback they might not get anywhere else.

Recognize good behavior with small, consistent steps. Things as minor as a student who always arrives on time allows your teachers to work more efficiently . . . so it counts. Staff who work behind the scenes to keep the bathrooms clean or the supply closet stocked help the school run smoothly . . . so it counts. Teachers who consistently give parents the information they need have a positive impact on academic success . . . so it counts. Parents who volunteer for special events reduce the workload for your staff . . . so it counts. Let them know it counts. Recognize good behavior!

TRUANCY TRUTHS

Maintain a firm grasp on truancy truths to fulfill unmet needs on campus and enhance community involvement.

Truancy is one of the most debilitating issues for students. Chronic absenteeism can lead to kids dropping out of school altogether. Even if they manage to graduate, students who skip too many classes end up in low-wage jobs or fail to find employment. Their lives are marred by poverty and dissatisfaction, especially when they are capable of so much more than they believe. A realistic approach to truancy truths empowers your school to prevent truancy before students lose too much class time while also reeling chronic offenders back to campus.

The truth about truancy is that a number of factors can trigger absences. In the home, poor supervision stemming either from weak parenting skills or the inability to supervise kids due to work schedules can result in skipped classes. Neighborhoods that aren't safe to walk through can prevent kids from arriving on campus on time or at all. Pressure to stay home to help out with family needs or even to take a job might steer students away from academics.

Other elements also contribute to absences. Teachers who aren't doing their best to reach every child can deflate the desire to learn. Bullying can make coming to school too painful for a child with few coping skills. Mental or physical health issues, ranging from depression to pregnancy, overwhelm educational needs with more immediate concerns. Low self-esteem or drug or alcohol use can make focusing difficult.

Fortunately, you have as many solutions at your disposal as there are problems. Teachers should take every absence seriously and connect with the student right away. Train your staff to probe gently by taking a caring tone and asking thoughtful questions. If the student doesn't respond well to that teacher, ask a person they connect with to step up. Don't forget that some kids will reach out to cafeteria workers, janitors, or clerks who don't represent authority figures. Make sure these staff have the same resources as your educators so they can help resolve truancy truths.

Children don't only get lost at school; they also fall through the cracks in other areas of life. Once you've shored up any elements that touch your campus, reach out to local organizations that might be able to help. Youth programs are a great way to place kids in a peer group that is inspired and goal-focused. Locate help for teenage mothers, educate parents about the lifelong benefits of supporting their kids' education, and pair students up with a buddy so they feel safe in their own neighborhoods. You'll deal with truancy truths in a holistic and effective manner.

VET VOLUNTEERS

Vetting volunteers develops a protocol that ensures your people are safe every time they interact with someone from outside the school.

Vettting volunteers prevents anyone with an inappropriate criminal background from interacting with your students or staff. When you have safeguards in place, individuals who might be predators, addicts, or who harbor other criminal intentions can't access the vulnerable population on campus.

Vetting volunteers is a national trend. The National School Safety Center reported that school volunteers are being subjected to criminal background checks more often to address fears about child molestation. The trend also stems from concerns over school liability for volunteers. Considering these very real issues, the only question is why a careful principal wouldn't require background checks!

Vet volunteers with compassion. Make sure your policy covers parents who might have felony convictions for nonviolent, nonyouth-related offenses like check fraud. Recognize that drug charges, especially old convictions, might not reflect the reality of a parent's current lifestyle. Since the National Sex Offender Registry is free to use and readily available online, your school can take a big step to keep students and staff safe.

DECIDE ON DISCIPLINE

Deciding on discipline allows you to implement clear and compassionate responses to behavioral issues in the student body.

Deciding on discipline provides clear guidelines and tells students what to expect if they do not meet the school's behavioral standards.

Disciplinary procedures lay out the consequences that will be faced immediately. They can also define the future potential impact of today's poor behavior.

Deciding on discipline isn't only about resolving conflict after the fact. Importantly, it creates a positive environment in which self-discipline, empathy, and accountability are valued and expected. Rather than having a zero-tolerance policy that broadcasts an inflexible—and seemingly uncaring—rule of law, deciding on discipline tailors the consequences to the circumstances. Along the way, you'll repair damaged relationships and avoid a disproportionate impact on students of color.

Decide on discipline before each academic year begins. This allows you to modify and adapt existing policies to address issues like higher arrest or suspension rates. With a more balanced approach, students know they'll be treated fairly. This enhances their motivation, which improves attendance and graduation rates as well as academic performance.

CURATE CURIOS

Curate curios from your staff to enhance relationships, build connections based on interests outside of academic areas, and make the workplace more interesting.

Curating curios is a process that invites educators, staff, and other personnel to provide a single object of interest to them. The object could be a catcher's mitt they use with a child on the weekends, a vintage cookie press, or a unique stone they found while walking along a river. Ask them to provide a paragraph about what they like about the object or why it holds meaning for them. Display the item and the description in the staff lounge for a short period before replacing it with something from a different person.

The kinds of objects that appear will run the gambit from common to surprising. The descriptions might talk about a person's relatives, their hobbies, or what they like to do to relax. The rotating displays offer your staff a moment or two to decompress with something fun. They'll likely learn something new about the people they work with every day, and that new knowledge will foster conversations and connections. The playfulness of the idea also lets people know that you're willing to think outside the box.

If dedicating a display area is too difficult, consider integrating a similar idea into staff meetings. You could open by displaying and discussing a unique object (with, of course, jokes about an adult version of show and tell). Pass out tiny plastic birds and ask educators to "act as free as a bird" for a day. Set up a scavenger hunt by hiding a $5 gift card in staff-only areas and releasing hints every week until it's found. Anything goes, really. By encouraging a sense of fun and excitement through curios not normally found in a school, you'll add to the many rewards that come from educational careers.

BANISH BULLIES

Banish bullies in the student body as well as on your staff to create a safe, supportive environment.

Banishing bullies allows your students to focus fully on their academic goals. When teachers who might bully students or peers are banished, the work environment becomes more productive. Parents who try to bully teachers and staff can weaken morale and deflect attention from the school's purpose, so ameliorating their impact keeps your school on track!

Banishing bullies who are adults can be difficult. In response to a GreatSchools article on teachers who were bullies, one teacher confessed to having bullied his special-ed students. He had just started teaching and was in his early twenties, a time when individuals might not have confidence in their own abilities. Faced with the extra challenges of teaching special-needs students, he responded in a terrible way. He was forced to resign . . . and eventually reformed his ways and returned to teaching as a supportive, caring adult.

Banish bullies in your student body by encouraging the targets to ignore the bully, report the person to an adult, or simply walk away. With teachers, counselors, or other staff, document the date, time, and details of every negative event. Investigate—quietly—incidences other adults might have noticed. Then sit down face to face to discuss the issue. In some cases, the adult might not even realize that his or her behavior is mean or unacceptable. If your teachers are being bullied by parents or cyberbullied by students, talk directly with the bullies. To prevent cyberbullying, ensure that teachers' computers and digital accounts are secured behind passwords and firewalls.

TRADE PLACES

Trading places encourages students, staff, and teachers to see the world through the eyes of others.

Trading places increases empathy and compassion on campus. It can reveal hidden challenges and develop a new sense of community and cooperation. Trading places can also be a fun way to engage with the many people you're responsible for!

Trading places can be fun when it's done in a very immediate manner. Have teachers select one of their students to lead the class for a single session. During that time, the teacher will sit at the student's desk. Assistance will of course be provided as needed! The exercise provides plenty of entertainment for the class while giving them a new way to look at what the teacher has to accomplish every day.

Trading places can be expanded beyond a Trade with the Teacher day. Students interested in cooking could help in the cafeteria for an hour. Those interested in sports could work with coaches. A parent could be offered the honor of helping in the administrative office for an afternoon or coaching the football team during a practice session. Afterward, have the participants and the staff they replaced write short essays. Share these experiences with the schools to spread the impact of the event.

STUDENTS HELPING STUDENTS

Schools that encourage students to help students support higher academic achievement while strengthening the campus community.

Students who help students bring a unique perspective to the table. They understand exactly the kinds of social and educational pressures being faced by their peers. They recognize the stress that comes from microaggressions and bullying, and can share their own experiences with these issues. When students help students study, they cement their own grasp of a curriculum while helping others advance academically.

And when young people see their peers reaching out to help, they feel more connected to the community on campus.

A number of different initiatives can open the door to students helping students. New arrivals to your campus can be teamed up with a buddy who shows them around school and helps them understand how things work. An afterschool tutoring program can match volunteers with individuals from their own or lower grades to work on specific lessons. Bilingual individuals can assist those for whom English is a second language with assignments and college applications.

The school can broadcast the expectation that all students will help students in the classroom. This is as simple as making it clear that, while in school, every student is responsible for ensuring that their peers are treated well by others. Ask students to look out for warning signs that their classmates might be depressed, anxious, using drugs, or suffering abuse at home. Young people often let their true selves show only when adults aren't around, so having their peers on the lookout will lead to a happier, safer, and healthier population.

Work throughout the year to connect students so they can help each other. Set up a day when everyone will spend the first hour interviewing a peer about their life. Enhance the interview by encouraging kids to share pictures they've taken of their family or places where they've lived. Once a month, assign the entire school a read-and-discuss article or essay about a young person who faced a challenge successfully. Open an online forum where students can post thoughts, concerns, and success stories related to the shared piece. By offering multiple ways for students to help students, your school will become a unified family with leaders rising out of the different grades.

CREATE A SURROGATE FAMILY

Create a surrogate family to reduce the impact of the home environment on motivation and academic achievement.

Creating a surrogate family reduces the number of in-school issues that stem from family life. By providing supportive attention, students know that someone cares . . . even if that care doesn't originate in their home. When students feel supported by peers and adults, they can focus more on academic achievement. Learning will help them escape their personal situations more quickly and with greater success!

Creating a surrogate family is something kids tend to do themselves. Every time a child turns to a counselor or teacher for advice, they're substituting that adult for a parent figure. When they make friends, they're filling the gap that might be left by an absent sibling. The school actually is a surrogate family for every child who walks through the doors! Creating these connections for kids who can't do it on their own brings everyone into the fold.

Create a surrogate family by connecting with the local Big Brother/ Big Sister organization. Locate youths who need the emotional and psychological support of a big brother or sister and connect the two. Many schools have student volunteers who mentor new transfers; connect these individuals with students who need a little extra support now and then. Allow parents who are so inclined to provide big brother/ big sister moments with students after school or during lunch.

INVEST IN HUMAN CAPITAL

Invest in human capital to focus on the teachers and staff who make the school everything it can be!

Investing in human capital recognizes that, although you are the leader, your employees implement the school's primary task: education. When you invest in your human capital, you ensure that every teacher is as strong as they can be. You pave the way for them to achieve even greater results, which generates academic excellence.

Investing in human capital is all about management. When you manage the very special people who have dedicated their lives to teaching, you communicate clear expectations. They understand that their principal isn't going to tuck away inside an office. Instead, everyone is part of their team. When their individual tasks feed into the greater whole, they constantly reinforce the importance of the school's success and their role in achieving that goal.

Invest in human capital by recruiting dedicated people. Recognize excellence wherever it appears and broadcast important milestones. At least once a year, conduct one-on-one meetings that give teachers a safe place to provide feedback and present new ideas. Respect their methods, especially ones that have proven successful, and discuss options for change when things don't work. Give your people the ability to provide input at every step and your human capital will grow by leaps and bounds!

GENDER DIVERSITY

Having a gender diversity framework in your school increases competency among your educators, promotes understanding on campus, and reduces the harassment experienced by nonbinary students and staff.

Even if you are already familiar with gender diversity, take a look at the most recent literature on the topic. A lot has changed since gender nonconformity began to be addressed in schools, and a lot more is likely to continue changing. The world has gone from recognizing only male and female genders to including transgender, gender neutral, agender, pangender, and other identities. Gender identity is a continuum, and like most continuums, it can be split down as finely as needed to include every person's perspective.

Recognize, and let others know, that any discomfort a person might feel when working with gender diverse students is far less important than providing fully inclusive educational opportunities. It is never acceptable for adults on campus to make negative remarks about gender expression. They might be called on one year to help a student transition between the social signals surrounding gender. Students should feel that every adult on campus will shield them from any adverse reactions from their peers.

Respect and active support are critically important in areas or activities that traditionally have been segregated by gender. Transgender and nonconforming students should always be given access to the facilities and teams that fit their identities. Their pronouns of choice and, if they've changed their name, their chosen name should be used when speaking with them or about them. Be an ally and an advocate. Encourage your people to become allies and advocates while they're on campus. Awareness combined with supportive action creates a fully inclusive school where every learner feels safe.

INCENTIVIZE, DON'T CRITICIZE

Incentivize don't criticize provides long-lasting rewards for performance and removes the negative thrust of penalties.

Incentivize don't criticize generates a safe, supportive environment. Rather than penalizing underperforming students or staff, incentives for strong performance encourage individuals to try new ways to succeed. Incentives eliminate the fear and distrust that can come from penalty-rich environments and focus people on the things that really count.

Incentivize don't criticize works best when the school's goals align with those of teachers. This approach also has a much more profound effect when offered to individuals rather than a group. Nonfinancial incentives like positive parental feedback and public coverage of milestones can be highly effective. Incentives enhance academic performance and the excellence of your school.

Incentivize don't criticize by using the tools already at hand. Send press releases to the local media about different milestones achieved by a certain class or group and be sure to showcase the teacher who led the initiative. Spread the word about ongoing success through social media pages and in-house news bulletins. Set up a teacher-of-the-month program and post pictures of that month's recipient in a prominent place. Always congratulate the individual in person. A handshake and a few words from you mean a lot!

INCLUSIVE BUDDIES

Pair student volunteers called inclusive buddies with individuals who have physical or learning disabilities to support comprehensive educational opportunities.

Peer buddy programs can handle a number of issues quite well. They call on a largely untapped resource, namely the student population, to help specific groups within that population. When you introduce inclusive buddies who focus on helping those with different types of disabilities, you pave a broad road for every student to achieve an education equal to that of other learners.

Inclusive buddies can function in a variety of situations. Naturally, your program will place most of the emphasis on classroom activities. Buddies can help other students work in small groups or respond to questions. They might explain assignments or make sure the individual understands what they're supposed to accomplish during that class period. The volunteer buddies might make sure a clear pathway awaits a student in a wheelchair, help them on with their coats at the end of the day, or perform other small tasks that allow the focus to stay on the teacher.

When buddies don't share all their class periods, additional buddies can help an individual arrive at their next class on time, store their things in their lockers, or carry their trays through the lunch line. Buddies might enter self-contained special education classes on a regular schedule to help those students work, grow, and learn. Others might team up during free periods or recess to engage in fun activities. In addition to making the school day easier for those with disabilities, the volunteers demonstrate, in a real and caring way, that every person is equal and equally deserving.

The students who volunteer to become inclusive buddies will develop their leadership skills. Often, they do more than help with tasks and assignments. They tend to introduce their partner into their own group of friends, expanding the opportunities for all the kids to connect on a level that fosters personal growth and understanding. When they work with individuals who struggle with learning disabilities, they boost academic success. The parents of these children will be grateful the school is so proactive. Your staff will be proud to be involved with a campus that harnesses meaningful ways to reach every learner.

EVERYONE IS A PROFESSIONAL

Everyone is a professional no matter what their role. Teachers, cooks, janitors, parents, and students are all professionals engaged in the careers of education, food service, maintenance, child-rearing, and learning.

Everyone is a professional allows you to recognize the value of every individual's role at your school. You'll create an atmosphere in which mutual respect is expected and delivered. Relationships are built on a foundation of trust; as a result, every individual becomes more engaged in the school's goals.

Treating everyone like a professional has its greatest impact on the diversity and inclusiveness of your school's culture. It overcomes the denigration aimed at low-skill jobs, low-income families, careers that have little political influence, and a host of other social ailments. Treating everyone like a professional proves that every person matters. When teachers, parents, and students carry that knowledge into the wider world, they are able to change the world!

Set the tone that everyone is a professional at your school. Talk to children about their "educational careers" to elevate their self-esteem. Place issues that seem to impact only one classroom in the context of the teaching profession. Recognize the role that parents hold as child-development professionals at home. When you approach everyone as professionals, they become more focused. They become motivated to achieve within their own careers!

Chapter 3

Wisdom for You

LEAD BY EXAMPLE

Leading by example means you guide others by demonstrating the activities and attitude you want throughout your school.

Leading by example touches on the core of your position at the school. As the head of the facility, you are not just a manager, you are a leader. An inclusive attitude, persistence in the face of daily challenges, and patience with all the minor annoyances that come with herding hundreds of kids toward educational goals inspires your staff to do the same. When others see the effort you put into every hour, they have a yardstick against which to measure their own efforts. Leading by example encourages others to step up, take on responsibilities above their job description, and rockets your school to success!

When you lead by example, you affirm that every person's job is as important as the other person's. You might, for example, fill in for a cafeteria manager or custodian when their sudden absence is unavoidable and no one else can perform their duties. Your effort sends a clear message about how highly you value those tasks. As a bonus, you can better assess the worth of their job and the daily challenges they face.

To lead by example, never ask an employee to do something you would not. Treat others as you would like to be treated—with courtesy, respect, and the dignity they deserve. Recognize people as your most valuable asset and express your appreciation often.

NEVER STOP LEARNING

Never stopping learning keeps you up to date with current research into educational methods and administrative procedures.

Never stopping learning isn't just a rallying cry for students . . . it's equally important for principals. When you position yourself on the cusp of new techniques and reaffirm the effectiveness of traditional methods, your perspective is broad enough to make wise choices. You'll also be innovative and discover the best improvements. It enhances your performance and your impact on teachers and students.

Never stopping learning is accessible right in your own school. Rather than call in outside experts, turn to ones in your school or district. After a regional conference, invite teachers and administrators throughout your state for an informal lunch to discuss the highlights. Create an internal forum where teachers and staff can post ideas, ask for advice, and glean the benefit of other people's experiences. As you help others, you'll reaffirm good practices in your own approach.

Many pathways help you to never stop learning. DVDs, podcasts, and web-based workshops can keep you abreast of the latest procedures. Engaging with online educational communities ties you into trending thoughts, opinions, and new ideas. Follow every conference or learning event by asking "What worked well?" "What didn't work as well as I'd hoped?" and "What could I have done differently?" When you never stop learning, every step propels you forward.

OWN MISTAKES

Owning mistakes recognizes that you're human and are occasionally going to misstep. While owning your own mistakes is important, you also have to own the mistakes of your teachers and staff. You are, after all, the leader. You are ultimately responsible for every mistake that happens inside your school.

Owning mistakes doesn't mean letting them weigh you down. Only when you deny or ignore mistakes will their weight accumulate—through distrust, loss of loyalty, and plummeting morale. When you own your mistakes and those of the school, you tell everyone the buck stops here . . . and the buck is going to be spent in a way that is productive and valuable.

Owning mistakes enhances your wisdom. When you miss a deadline or underperform because you're juggling too many responsibilities, you discover that you need to delegate more. If you hear that a sterling teacher is thinking about leaving because of some administrative snafu, you might recharge that teacher's passion by having him or her create solutions. And for those moments when your own commitment wavers, you can step back and reassess the situation.

Owning mistakes doesn't have to be a huge production. A simple apology to someone who feels slighted followed by a short conversation can do wonders for morale. E-mails to parents who are unhappy about procedures can minimize how often individuals lash out at your teachers. Accepting that a mistake was made and then taking measurable steps to address the issue is always the best policy.

DIGITAL DETOX

Treat yourself to frequent digital detoxes to reduce stress, clear your mind, and become more efficient.

The different technologies that have entered our lives provide a host of benefits. Unfortunately, they also come with a slew of negative impacts. Being constantly connected to the workplace and, for principals, tracking the social media and traditional media coverage of their districts ramps up the stress. When you plan time for a digital detox, you provide yourself with much needed downtime. You give yourself the space to clear away worries, step away from anxieties, and return to your campus refreshed. You might also find that you'll sleep better and that your interactions with people grow warmer and more satisfying.

To implement the most effective digital detox, break your digital time down into two components. First is the element that brings information in from outside. This includes social media (that of other schools), news websites, informative programs, and training classes. The second element encompasses communication channels like e-mail, texts, and video conferencing; this also includes your school's social media feeds. Principals will find this approach particularly useful because they need to use their devices every day.

Consider the group of information channels. Use your browser history to discover which sites you visit most often. Think about why you're checking each site, and pare down your list so that you only visit those that truly provide benefit. As you make cuts, be particularly ruthless with sites you scroll through because the content relaxes you. Instead of shaking off tension by continuing to stare at a screen, substitute an activity that requires a different type of activity. A quick walk or a few in-chair stretches can work wonders.

Once you have a shortlist of premium sites, the ones you truly need to view, schedule a time during which you'll check in. Your visits might be daily for the websites that provide rapid updates, and weekly for ones that refresh their content less frequently. Don't exceed your time limit, even by a few minutes. You'll likely discover that you benefit just as much with the curtailed viewing as you did with more extensive scrolling. Remember to manage your list moving forward. If you add a site, try to find a different one you can remove. You'll curate your information sources and become far more efficient.

The communication element is a bit difficult to manage, but success is still within reach. Start by breaking your types of communication down into subsets ranked by importance. Updating and checking social media, for example, can wait until the end of the day. E-mails that arrive from parents might be answered in fifteen-minute blocks before and after lunch. Reduce the number of video meetings you attend, if possible, or turn the camera off so you can sort paperwork (or even take a walk) while listening in. Use the tools built into your e-mail software to notify you when priority messages arrive; otherwise, only check your e-mail twice a day. After only a week or two, these digital detoxes will leave you with more energy to address things that really matter.

LEAD WITH INTEGRITY

When you lead with integrity, you do the right thing because it's the right thing to do.

Leading with integrity provides your school with the stability that comes from having a courageous leader at the helm. Integrity encourages others to mirror your example and take action to right a wrong.

Finally, it models integrity for others who aren't your employees like students and parents.

Integrity can change in subtle yet important ways depending on the community in which your school resides. It's important, therefore, to define leading with integrity as a concept that honors the mores and values of your community. Whenever you defend your students against unfair disciplinary actions, you're leading with integrity. Every time you go to the mat for a teacher's raise or promotion, you're leading with integrity. And when the groups who fancy themselves watchdogs of education start making outrageous demands, your integrity is the first line of defense for the school.

Lead with integrity every day. Encourage individuals to actually avail themselves of your open-door policy. Hire individuals who have a demonstrable history of high ethical standards. Confront anyone whose behavior violates the integrity of your school. Eliminate gossip at every level and replace it with factual information.

TAKE CALCULATED RISKS

Anytime you step outside your comfort zone to try something new, you risk failing. Depending on the risk, failure might cost you time, effort, money, or even respect. A calculated risk, on the other hand, is one you've thought through. You've weighted the potential gain against the potential loss and found the ratio acceptable.

Calculated risks can open up new worlds. They allow you to explore different paths and discover unique ways to address old challenges. Calculated risks, even when they fail, bring fresh air into a stagnant culture. They break old habits that might be blocking the perfect solution. Calculated risks push you and your school to achieve more.

Calculated risks are ingrained in the educational process. Students are asked every day to step outside of their comfort zone and learn something new. Teachers are constantly asked to upgrade and enhance their skills and abilities with training and development sessions. Every time you ask your staff to work at their maximum ability—and a bit beyond—you're taking a calculated risk. You're balancing growth against comfortable routines. Even if you fail, you've set the performance bar high . . . and you've encouraged everyone to strive for those goals.

The nature of calculated risks makes them a little scary. If you're considering a large or unusual risk, all the calculation in the world might not prevent failure. Instead of going all in, break the risk down into smaller pieces. Take a single step. Study it to see what worked and what didn't. Revise your original plan then take that step again. When it succeeds, implement the next portion of the plan. Repeat and achieve by calculating and reducing the risk.

FIND A MENTOR

A mentor is a person who agrees to share experience, knowledge, skills, and ability with someone else in their field.

Finding a mentor gives you a leg up on a very complex job. A mentor can speed your progress through different learning curves, encourage you to implement your ideas, fill in gaps in your knowledge, and provide a space in which you can engage in collaborative and reflective learning. Mentors can provide fresh perspectives and detailed advice as well as broad support. Best of all, mentors can listen when you need a friendly ear.

Mentors can be particularly helpful when budgets force staff cuts. Educational professionals frequently enter the field because they have a passion for teaching, so retired professionals might be willing to mentor you without the need for funding. And since mentoring focuses on how rather than why, it relies on anecdotal elements rather than research. Books, your network, and internet discussion boards can stand in for a mentor when time or direct access is limited.

In some states, mentors are available through formalized programs. The principal who held your position before you can be tapped; just ask if they'd be willing to provide guidance now and then. Principals at nearby schools are another source. And now that technology allows us to communicate instantly with video feeds and e-mails, you might locate mentors in different states. Although mentors are usually considered a way to prepare a new principal for the road ahead, they can support a principal at any point during their career.

GET GRIT

When principals get grit, they supercharge their progress toward long-term goals with one of the top predictors of success.

We've been taught to think of intellect and experience as the key pathways to achieving goals. When you get grit, though, you develop a positive state of mind that supports your efforts with a blend of passion and persistence. Grit springs from, and supports, a deep commitment to persevere. The bravery and stamina you develop is one of your best aids as you work your way through the challenges presented by various plans and activities.

Although the definition of grit can come off sounding a little hard-nosed, it's actually tied directly to character. However you define a strong character—by laying out a defined set of values, for example, or by focusing on heart-centered actions—grit is often found in individuals we look to as models of good character. If your level of determination isn't enough to tackle the difficult times, or if it's not channeling pleasure during the good times, you can still develop this mind-set and get grit.

First, show up. Don't just arrive physically to your campus; arrive mentally and emotionally. Every time you step onto campus, look around. Smell the air. Notice a detail you've never seen before, or spend just one minute closely studying an item you would normally skim past. This will help you arrive fully. You'll be present in the moment and ready to start your day.

Once a week, compete with yourself. Pick a task and set a goal like *today, I will complete this update in less time than I did before.* You might also tweak the areas where you want to enhance your skills. If you want to connect more easily with parents, for example, your goal might be *as I greet parents, I will hold eye contact for five seconds.* These tiny steps will yield surprisingly large impacts. You'll feel better about your progress, which will enhance your ability to bring your best to your work every day. You'll strengthen your personal reserve of grit.

BALANCE WORK AND HOME

Balancing work and home means that one never consumes the other. Your career, while meaningful, doesn't reduce your enjoyment of your personal life. At the same time, your personal challenges and goals don't undermine your career.

When you balance work and home, you reap the best of both worlds. You arrive at school recharged, refreshed, and able to tackle the complex mix of a principal's day. When you return home, you're able to leave behind any frustration or anxiety because the pleasures you derive from family and friends rounds out the fullness of you as a human being.

All things have a time. Balancing work and home allows you to address each challenge and new opportunity at the proper time and in a positive way. When work and home are balanced, you live a lifestyle that has integrated your personal goals and your professional aspirations. As you move forward in one area, you find the passion and inspiration to move forward in the other. You become an integrated human being.

Balancing work and home doesn't mean you'll divide your time or effort neatly between the two. At times, you might focus more on your career by taking developmental courses, traveling to conferences, and following other opportunities. When things at school are moving smoothly, you might take a vacation, attend to family needs, or engage in hobbies. Shifting your attention to match new goals provides you with a true balance that, over time, enhances all areas of your life!

NETWORK

It's lonely at the top. Networking cultivates relationships that allow you to become more productive. These relationships support you within a group of peers.

Networking is a wise move for principals. A select group can provide you with the information you need more quickly than the research you undertake on your own. Networks convey the experiences of decades or even lifetimes. Individuals can point you in new directions, connect you with other individuals, and uncover hidden resources.

Networking among principals ultimately benefits the students. At the University of Los Angeles, the Educational Evaluation Group conducted a nationwide study of school leader networks. The confidence principals gained through this type of support improved student outcomes. And Massachusetts high schools led by networked principals outperformed state graduation rates.

To network, join local and national education organizations. Attend conferences and workshops, give presentations or start up a blog, and always have a business card handy. Social media is a great place to expand your reach into a group of like-minded people. Whenever you come across an article or publication you like, reach out to the author or the experts who were quoted. You'll build a strong network with individuals whose skills and experiences can help you achieve your goals.

FEED YOUR PASSION

Passion is the spark that motivates you as a principal. Feeding your passion engages you in activities that absorb you and that lend meaning to your career.

Nearly everyone who works in education is passionate about what they do. But principals aren't your average educator. Instead of working directly with students, they've stepped up to a broader viewpoint that allows them to help students while helping teachers. Feeding your passion will have wide-reaching effects that benefit everyone involved with your school.

Feeding your passion begins the day you start as a principal. It continues whenever you face challenges with the determination and focus your passion generates. When your students and staff excel, your passion is fed because their successes are your own. Interacting with parents feeds your passion because they see the fruits of your labor in their children.

Feed your passion every day. Pick up a book on people who've made a difference in their communities . . . because you are one of those people. Recognize that every time you hire a new teacher or evaluate another, you're enhancing how students learn. As you walk the grounds, consider the machine that has grown under your leadership. Feeding your passion generates a self-sustaining loop of support that feeds your passion even more!

CUT OFF COMPASSION FATIGUE

The intensity of the effort involved with helping others can affect the giver negatively. Cut off compassion fatigue in order to support everyone on your campus over the long run.

Compassion fatigue is often mistaken for burnout. While both involve feeling tired and dissatisfied, compassion fatigue is directly related to the trauma suffered by the people you help. Principals, therapists, and medical professionals are all, due to the nature of their jobs, vulnerable to this type of stress. Long hours, truly caring for others, and experiencing grief when you hear the details of their suffering combine into a form of traumatic stress. Being aware of compassion fatigue is your first step toward cutting it off.

Whenever you start to feel down, or when you notice your own mood swings, lack of motivation, or an unwillingness to spend time with family and friends, check into whether you need to cut off compassion fatigue. You might also experience physical symptoms like exhaustion, changes in appetite, or headaches. Because some of these same symptoms can point to depression or burnout, it's important to know that compassion fatigue might very well be the cause.

Self-care is your number one way to cut off compassion fatigue. The more you recharge your inner source of caring, the more you'll be able to draw on that source to care for others. Just about any of the tips in this section will prevent you from getting to the point where you just can't care for others in the same way. If you find that you're already showing symptoms, block out time to consider what's truly important to you. Then reconnect with those important things. If relatives are important, make time to engage with them meaningfully. Focus on the children you brought into this world and who make you so proud. Experiencing the depth of feelings that surround these important areas of your life will reset your balance.

If you need a little push to make time for what's important, talk through your difficulties with someone you trust. In this case, seek out someone who's also in the educational field. They'll understand many of the issues you have without needing long explanations. Speaking your intentions to focus on things you value will spark your passion to follow through. Since meaningful conversations are one of the ways to cut off compassion fatigue, seek out one of these interactions every single day. You'll keep yourself well away from the stress zone and you'll be well ahead of the game.

TRUST YOUR INTUITION

Intuition is that quick flash of understanding that comes without having to think things through. Trusting your intuition will very rarely steer you wrong.

Although intuition appears to be completely removed from logical processing, it is actually based on your broad experiences. Instead of coming through the conscious mind, however, it flies up from the subconscious. Trust your intuition to access a different kind of knowledge. Whereas your intellect lays out rational elements, intuition is formed from the wisdom that comes from integrating facts and information with experiences.

Trust your intuition to resolve things that seem too complex for your intellectual mind to track. This is particularly important for principals because they so often deal with situations where all the information isn't available. A student or teacher's personal beliefs, events they experienced in the past, and their true motives impact how they behave. These elements are frequently hidden from you . . . and sometimes are even hidden from the mind that harbors those elements! When you trust your intuition, you allow your wisdom to resolve issues without having to dig up things that might remain hidden despite your best efforts.

You can trust your intuition in nearly every aspect of your job. Pay attention to that tingle at the back of your neck while you're listening to someone's explanation; it could be telling you that something's not right about what they're saying. Feel whether someone's nervousness is because they're hiding something or merely because you represent authority. The more often you allow your intuition to inform your intellect, the faster you'll be able to judge situations and make the right decision.

HAVE FUN!

Have fun might sound like a strange bit of wisdom, but it's not. Learning is exciting! Schools are huge mixing pots where individuals from all age groups and backgrounds interact. Having fun means opening yourself to the delightful moments.

Having fun benefits you and everyone around you. When you enjoy the accomplishments of others and even silly student antics, you engage in the fullness of the educational process. When others see that you're open to delight, they open themselves to those moments. As people share positive anecdotes, stress is relieved and people become more relaxed. The environment feels safe and open.

Having fun really motivates students. The National Association of Elementary School Principals proposes that principals do whatever it takes to enliven the learning atmosphere. Some of the activities their proposal inspired were truly outrageous. Principals shaved their heads, allowed students to dye their hair with the school's colors, kissed a calf, kissed a pig, and hung out on the roof. Integrating fun into your job helps your school!

Having fun is accessible in every moment. Liven up your e-mail updates to teachers by inviting an artistic student to submit a cartoon. Swap roles with someone for a day and share the funny moments with the entire student body. Always participate in dress-up days with your own costumes and never be afraid to act silly!

PRACTICE A SPIRITUAL LIFE

Practicing a spiritual life brings interconnectedness, authenticity, and meaning to your career.

Practicing a spiritual life enhances how you perform at your job as well as how others view your performance. When you reach out across cultural, social, and other boundaries, you achieve interconnectedness at your school. When you strive for an authentic connection between your personal values and the ones you implement at school, you demonstrate integrity. When your internal life aligns with your efforts as a principal, you generate meaning. All these results are noticed by teachers, students, and parents. You become greater in their eyes . . . and more deeply human.

Practicing a spiritual life isn't about applying the rules governing your own beliefs to the school environment. Instead, it's about enhancing the positive aspects of education through nuanced activities. When you demonstrate fairness and honesty in your inner self, the people at school know you are trustworthy. By becoming a leader who serves with humility and respect, individuals are encouraged to model your behavior.

No matter how you define the practice of a spiritual life, your actions can benefit your school. The best way is through a spiritual filter. Define the three primary tenants of your spiritual beliefs. These might be integrity, fairness, and service. Then, whenever you reach out to troubled students or are approached for help, filter your response through those three components. When you weigh your options on that scale, you'll easily discover which approach is best . . . and you'll lead in a spiritual way.

TAMING PARENTS

In aggressively parent-oriented communities, taming parents helps school administrators focus on academic goals, reduces stress among teachers, and ensures equal access for all students.

Every school will have a handful of parents who take up an inordinate amount of time. Often, these same individuals will demand concessions or special treatment for their children that just isn't warranted. Taming parents is a skill that every principal will have to apply at some point in their professional careers. But when a handful of parents turns into an entire community of aggressive individuals, you have to level up with skills that help you manage group dynamics.

In most cases, the approaches you implemented when dealing with individual parents can be easily modified to address groups. Listening, for example, goes far in any situation. Rather than meeting individually with every parent or pair of parents to listen to concerns, consider setting up a task force. Require all suggestions, complaints, and other input to flow through the task force. This allows you to focus on your administration tasks while a small, handpicked crew runs interference.

Better yet, hand that chore to the community. Ask them to set up an association similar to a PTA group that will liaison between the school and the parents. The group will deal with the intensive time required to hear every individual speak. Importantly, when the community task force and parents discuss issues, the feedback and opinions of peers can eliminate some of the outrageous demands. When individuals see how fellow parents respond to their "my kid first" asks, you're less likely to hear about them.

Be sure to provide at least one purely social event for the public every year. An aggressive community tends to look at everyone who works on campus as an obstacle to their child's best interests. When you pull everyone together—and I mean everyone, from the maintenance staff up to the district administrators—parents will begin to recognize you and your staff as human beings. They'll discover ways to connect with you that don't have anything to do with academics. Some of those parents will discover that you're actually on their side. And when it comes to interpersonal dynamics, a crumb can be baked into a nourishing loaf.

BE RELIABLE

Being reliable means that, no matter how exciting or chaotic the situation, people can turn to you.

Being reliable creates a safe environment. Everyone who walks through the doors in the morning knows what to expect. Because they have that stability, they are free to focus on the task at hand and to try new things. Your reliability is their anchor.

Being reliable is about keeping your promises. More so, it's about maintaining an even course. When you assign tasks, don't change the goal without a reason . . . and when you do, be sure everyone knows why the goal shifted. Consistency helps teachers clear away worries and devote their attention to their students. Parents worry less because their experiences with the school have been consistent. Students are free to reach further because the ground beneath them won't shift unexpectedly.

Reliability is created by your actions and your procedures. Policies that govern student behavior should be set at the beginning of the year and clearly communicated. Expectations should be communicated to the entire staff and reiterated to individuals who need occasional reminders. Procedures should be transparent. Reliability keeps the foundation of your school from being shaken by exterior elements because the school has its own internal stability.

Implement reliability into everything you touch. Attend meetings where your presence is important or communicate early that your representative will be there in your stead. Follow up even on casual comments about issues. And always demonstrate to the students that you are reliably consistent, fair, and appropriate.

CULTIVATE FORGIVENESS

Cultivating forgiveness is the deliberate act of healing the negative emotions that result from an offense, slight, or mistake.

Cultivating forgiveness will reduce your frustration over the issues you face in the course of your job. Cultivating forgiveness in your people allows them to relinquish their negative feelings and find peace. When you demonstrate true forgiveness on a regular basis, you're more likely to be forgiven when you fail to meet someone's expectations . . . whether those expectations are fair or not!

Cultivating forgiveness is an almost daily activity. Too often, minor transgressions pile up until one more simply becomes too much. By releasing each as it occurs, you eliminate the burden of witnessing so many small transgressions throughout the day. Forgiveness for larger offenses is important because you recognize that major offenses occur only infrequently. You find peace and become more balanced and proactive.

Cultivating forgiveness doesn't mean you ignore or forget the transgression. You will always have to correct the situation to properly manage the school and the student body. Cultivating forgiveness does allow a clearer perspective. The clearer your perspective becomes, the sooner you'll be able to clear out your frustration through forgiveness. The upward spiral carries your teachers and students as it lifts you!

PRESENT YOURSELF

Presenting yourself allows you to be perceived as actively engaged with the school.

Presenting yourself shows that you care. Students recognize that the person in authority isn't only interested in rules and enforcement. Teachers recognize an individual who steps outside the confining office to see what's really going on. Support staff realize that every element of the school, even those maintained through menial jobs, is important.

Presenting yourself as actively engaged extends your reach off campus. Connecting with politicians and regional leaders interested in educational programs brings your school to their attention. It conveys the message that you are open to their programs. Presenting yourself to outside organizations also expands your network, opening up new worlds for your teachers and your students.

Present yourself every day. Hang out at different school entrances during the morning rush as parents drop off their children. Cruise the teacher break room now and then to strike up a conversation with whoever happens to be present. Wander into the auditorium when the choral group or the theater group is rehearsing. E-mail reporters to comment on articles they've written about education and ask nonprofit groups how they might enhance the educational experience at your school. Each of these small efforts adds up to a powerful presentation of an engaged, caring leader.

FEED YOUR FRIENDS

Feed your friends on campus and in your personal life to enhance your professional experiences and enjoy pleasant experiences.

When you feed your friends, recognize that principals have at least two types. One set lives at work, or is in some way associated with your workplace. This group might include district managers, teachers from other schools, or principals in another state. The second set consists of people you've met through private activities, and includes neighbors, people in groups you've joined, and relatives.

Broadly speaking, all your friends can be nurtured with one of your most precious gifts: attention. Time isn't really part of the equation. Ten minutes spent truly listening is worth so much more than an hour of distracted engagement. Short exchanges that are fun or unique can bolster ties when you can't break away, so send a quick text thanking them for being your friend or e-mail a digital card just to say hello. When you do have time, drop off their favorite snack at their house or bring them cut flowers from your garden. Any small gesture works because it's a tangible symbol of how much you value them.

Feeding friends at work can be a little more complex. If your friends aren't directly associated with your campus, you can connect with them as you might with anyone in your personal life. When the individual is directly involved in your workday, however, you must maintain your leadership role and avoid the appearance of favoritism. With work friends, your gestures should be made in private or through private channels. Avoid giving gifts of any kind, no matter how small, at your workplace if your friend will be the only recipient. When you meet this person off campus, you can freely exchange holiday gifts or offer them something fun.

The efforts associated with feeding friends at work and in your private life shouldn't feel like a burden. Every time you focus on them, you receive a moment of relaxation, pleasure, and fun. Beyond that moment, having and holding friendships will make you feel cared for. The people you hold dear will respond in kind, creating an upward cycle of give and take that benefits you both.

CONSERVE YOUR TIME

Conserving your time consciously controls and manages the time you spend on specific activities.

Conserving your time makes you more effective, efficient, and productive. You'll reduce the amount of time spent on meaningless tasks and trim the amount of time spent on less important ones. You'll be able to focus on the important issues. You'll also become more accessible to students, teachers, and parents.

The complexity of a principal's job makes conserving your time critical. Generally, recognize that your duties fall into three general categories: thoughts, conversations, and actions. One of these is going to be a natural for managing with a calendar. You might schedule conversations only during certain hours, for example, or schedule five minutes of downtime after every conversation to take notes.

Everyone nowadays feels overwhelmed by demands. Conserve your time by delegating, calling on your network, and giving yourself time to reflect. Although scheduling things can be helpful, flexibility is one key to conserving your time. If you end up engaged in a task or conversation that doesn't actually require your input, excuse yourself. Affirm to others that they're well equipped to achieve the goal and hand off the responsibility with confidence. Conserving your time allows others to shine!

KEEP A JOURNAL

Keep a journal as a tool for reflection, reminders, and stress relief.

Keeping a journal is a low-cost, fast, and effective way to manage a number of issues principals face. You can jot down various tasks you need to remember or follow-ups that have to be scheduled. Enter a description of the day's highlights so that you can leave your work behind when you go home. Write about the week's accomplishments before the weekend to review the advances you've generated with all that effort!

When you've decided to keep a journal, earmark a certain amount of time on a regular basis. Select a quiet, private space in which to work. Start with jotting down reminders. This clears your mind of all the nagging chores and allows you to go deeper. Then spend five minutes (or more) writing. One day you might focus on a challenging event; the next, you might write about a success. The greatest results will come when you write about ongoing elements. With each entry, you'll put things in order, gain clarity, and come closer to answers.

Most people keep a journal in writing. To prevent hacking of digital journals, use your personal laptop or tablet. A handwritten journal will prevent the information from being stolen even from your personal device. It might be easier to use the dictation option on your devices to dictate the entries, record audio files, or even videotape your thoughts.

ENGAGE IN THE RIGHT FIGHT

Engaging in the right fight is about choosing where and how to spend your effort and your social capital.

Engaging in the right fight allows you to focus on the events and activities that will provide the greatest benefits. It avoids leadership that appears to champion change for change's sake and builds trust in your wisdom. When you engage in the right fight, you allow ideas that aren't feasible or that simply won't work to die naturally. Engaging in the right fight increases the success of your school!

Engaging in the right fight is something you can watch on television. CNN has an eight-episode documentary called *Chicagoland* about Principal Liz Dozier's efforts in an environment where 92 percent of the student population is from low-income families and 31 percent is classified as homeless. In four years, the school's graduation rate has nearly doubled and serious misconduct has decreased.

Whenever you are presented with an issue or a challenge, engage in the right fight by asking yourself three things: Will engaging in this effort positively impact one or more of our goals? Can this effort be accomplished with current resources? Will the results equal or outweigh the resources required? If the answer to all three is yes, move ahead. If your current resources are insufficient but the idea is good, revisit it when circumstances change. If it won't meet at least one goal or will cost more than it's worth, let it pass.

COPE WITH CHANGE

The constantly transforming educational system, from your campus up to the federal level, challenges principals to cope with change.

We all know that change can be challenging. Most of us tend to consider only the technical aspects of change, like having to use different forms or shuffle schedules. It's important to recognize that change also involves intangible psychological aspects. The best way to cope with change, then, is to break down your options into the three basic pathways: flight, fight, or flow. These three options define the core ways humans initially react to change. By tapping into this instantaneous response, you'll be prepared to deal with the technical and the emotional impacts.

Flight, for example, usually isn't an option. However, you can help individuals flee from intolerable changes by moving students between classrooms, adjusting teacher rosters, or making other modifications. Your goal is to move those individuals who truly can't manage the new methods into areas where their existing skills can be utilized best. You're helping them feel comfortable and safe, and you're still moving the school forward. Everyone will feel more accepting of the change. Everyone wins.

Fight, on the other hand, is often an option, and I mean this in the most positive way. Sometimes you will rally against a change and roll things back to the way they were. More often, however, you will want to modify proposed changes so they'll fit your school's needs. Ask where the new rules allow for wiggle room. Ask how much leeway you have in terms of scheduling. And, when an edict arrives that allows for zero adjustments, find ways to implement the change with the least disruption to your campus. You'll be fighting in a good way. No matter the final result, you'll have approached the change with the focus squarely on what's best for your school.

Then there's flow. When you meet a change with flow, you're going with what you're given. Either the change is recognized as an improvement, or there's simply no way to adjust the expectations or rules associated with the new method. In this case, do your best to convey a relaxed attitude. Meeting the challenge as you would any other task diffuses a lot of the tension. A relaxed attitude will help your educators implement the modifications without resenting the extra work involved.

KNOW WHERE YOU'RE GOING

Knowing where you're going provides the confidence that, while the map might change, you'll always move closer to your goals.

Knowing where you're going provides you with a clear and definite end goal. It becomes a beacon that shines light on the smaller steps needed to reach the goal. Whenever things seem overwhelming, you can always look toward the beacon and know that the effort will pay off. When you tell others where you're going, they're able to head for the same beacon. They might take a different path or use a different vehicle, but you'll arrive together!

Knowing where you're going is easy to define, but it's not always easy to execute. The route to your goal might not be clear. In some cases, you'll have to spend considerable time searching for the right pathway. You'll start down one road and discover it heads for a bog. You'll change paths and end up in a meadow that, although beautiful, doesn't provide the fruit you seek. When you know where you're going, how you get there doesn't matter. It only matters that you keep pressing forward down any available path.

Know where you're going every day. Every Monday, consider what you want to accomplish during the coming week. Jot down the most important places you want to go. Recognize that your arrival times might not match your calendar—you might arrive at one goal early and another goal late—and that's all right. As long as you know where you're going, you can be confident in your ability to get there!

EARN RESPECT

Earning respect is a reminder that, while the most effective leaders respect others for who and what they are, you frequently will need to prove your worth before others offer respect.

Earning respect is the keystone of your tenure as a principal. Without the respect of your staff, your students, and their parents, your ability to move your school in the right direction will crumble. Earning the respect of your teachers strengthens teamwork. Earning the respect of students strengthens learning. And earning the respect of parents enhances compliance with off-campus activities that boost academic success.

Earning respect is nowhere more important than with your teachers. They are the backbone of the school and perform much of the heavy lifting of lesson implementation, state mandate compliance, and learning. When teachers respect their leader, they work for you as well as the students. And whenever one teacher hears another undermine your authority, they'll support you in the moment when it counts the most!

Earn respect through consistent efforts. When you approach issues, remove any personal tinge from the discussion and stay focused on the challenge. Turn attention toward the solution rather than dwelling on the problem. Respond quickly, express sympathy in demanding circumstances, and assess without judging the individuals involved. And if you notice anyone acting in a less than respectful manner toward others, take immediate action. Creating a culture of mutual respect is one of the best ways to earn respect.

SPARK YOUR INSPIRATION

Sparking your inspiration is a motivational tool that keeps you functioning at your highest level.

Spark your inspiration to carry you through the bad times . . . and to fully enjoy the good times! When you're inspired, you can cut through all the clutter that fills your thoughts. You'll focus on the things that truly matter and achieve your goals with less stress. And when the important things are achieved more easily, the smaller details fall into place.

Sparking your inspiration isn't something principals often think about. So much material focuses on inspiring teachers, students, and parents that we tend to forget to inspire principals! An inspired leader demonstrates the positive attitude and dedication others need to trust their leader. When the principal is inspired, more gets done . . . not just by the person in charge but by everyone.

Spark your inspiration by trying new things . . . and not just at school. Invite new activities and people into the whole of your life. Take up a hobby, read a different type of book than you usually would, or visit a new attraction in your area one weekend every month. The more you add, the brighter your ideas for your school will become. By following up on those ideas, you'll discover new opportunities and new pathways to your goals. Get out, have fun, and spark your own inspiration!

COMMUNITY CARE

Engage in community care to make a difference, meet people, learn new skills, and become part of a group outside the school's doors.

Volunteering for activities related to community care offers a host of benefits. While you're pitching in to help others, you'll contribute to the bonds that hold your community together. You'll achieve deep satisfaction from seeing the good your efforts accomplish. You'll build your existing network with individuals who work outside your field, and you'll connect with people who hold similar values. If your community project involves physical activity, you'll garner better physical fitness in the bargain.

The opportunities to participate in community care programs are so varied that you're bound to discover one that aligns with your passions. Soup kitchens always need help with food preparation and service. Because religious and spiritual organizations often run multiple activities and can afford only a limited staff, their need for volunteers is high. You might try a summer camp to get a dose of sunshine while you mentor kids, or you can help build low-cost homes. If you want to do something on a drop-in basis, you can still engage in community care. Adopt an area of your neighborhood park to keep clean and tidy. Stop by the local food shelter and offer to sort food or hand out groceries during one shift.

The sense of purpose that results from community care is the perfect counterpoint to the stress principals often carry. Being part of something bigger than yourself gives meaning to your life. The tasks you'll undertake can be very different from what you're used to, so the challenge of learning new things will stimulate your intellect. You might also find that new skills associated with marketing, public speaking, or fundraising will be useful at school for current or future efforts. Even without these very real benefits, volunteering will take you to new places, introduce you to new ideas, and leave you fulfilled. The good deeds will make you happy, especially when they are received with gratitude. In some ways, community care can be the best type of self-care.

KNOW OTHER LEADERS

Knowing other leaders prompts you to discover who the informal leaders are among your teachers, within the student body, and in the larger community.

Knowing other leaders creates different opportunities for you to get things done. Informal leaders evoke trust, inspire confidence, and command respect. When you pull informal leaders into your sphere of influence, you are better able to evoke trust, inspire confidence, and command respect from the groups they lead.

Knowing other leaders is something you've probably already done. There's always one parent whose voice seems to influence the parent organizations even though that person has no official role. This person might be the same informal leader for all the parents' efforts, or this person might only "lead" certain activities. Either way, you've probably already been in a situation where winning the group means winning that person's support.

Know other leaders by recognizing that informal leaders aren't singled out in any formal way. Instead, they're people whose peers consider them valuable enough to follow. Among students, look for the individual who spurs others to achieve more . . . whether in positive or negative ways. Recognize that an informal leader might not be close to authority; in fact, informal leadership can easily develop around someone who is so removed from authority they seem powerless. Once you've identified them, convey your message, goals, or vision as clearly as possible. Then let them decide where they stand on the issue. Honor their influence as you would have them honor yours to achieve the most from informal leaders.

ENERGETIC ENTHUSIASM

Energetic enthusiasm charges the atmosphere within your school.

Energetic enthusiasm impacts everyone associated with your school. When you display energetic enthusiasm, students know that their performance and behavior counts every minute. Teachers and staff understand that their contributions, from the smallest grounds-keeping task to the highest educational aspirations, help build the school. Parents recognize that their students are shepherded by a group of individuals who care deeply about their children's future.

Energetic enthusiasm shines through you. Every interaction should emphasize your positive feelings about the school and its achievements. The principal who shares negative information with the wrong people undermines the atmosphere of the school. The principal who focuses on the positive—even when addressing challenges or resolving issues—motivates, inspires, and creates a school that shines!

Display energetic enthusiasm every time you interact with people. Recognize that mistakes and problems are opportunities to learn and grow. Champion challenges, recognize efforts to address the challenges, and then move on quickly to keep your school on track. Successful projects, efforts that are implemented smoothly, and operational efficiency all provide opportunities for energetic enthusiasm. Focus on the positive for a positive educational experience!

DECIDE AND ABIDE

Decide and abide means you measure the worth of an idea, make a judgment, and then support the decision and its results.

Decide and abide allows your school to move forward. Rather than having everything in an unknown status—which makes people nervous—decisions made for or against any particular initiative settles the issue. Individuals can progress knowing where the boundaries are and how they are expected to act. Your confident decision-making gives teachers, students, and parents the confidence to focus on the educational experience.

The best example of decide and abide in action is demonstrated by a mistake. Let's say you decide not to move forward with a particular initiative. You abide by that decision until events or other information prove your decision was incorrect. You then make a new decision on the basis of better information and abide by the new choice. Mistakes can be corrected. Indecision, on the other hand, creates instability and fear. Indecision has no place in your school.

Decide and abide using the best information at hand. Take input from your trusted advisors, consider teachers' viewpoints, and check in with how students and parents might respond. Base your decision on the most accurate predictions and let everyone know what you've chosen. Abide by your decision on new initiatives by providing resources and support. Abide by your decision not to implement other projects by reviewing your decision when new information appears. You'll display confidence with each decision and serenity as you abide with each decision. Both encourage individuals to trust your wisdom!

WHEN TO RETIRE

Knowing when to retire allows principals to plan for the good of their schools as well as their own good.

Too often, principals retire when they no longer look forward to their jobs. The lack of support, lack of funding, and lack of so many other critical elements wears on them and sends them out the door. But knowing when to retire for all the right reasons gives you a much healthier outlook on your career. When you plan the last phase of your educational career, you'll leave behind a school that is healthy, high functioning, and a great place to work.

Before you arrive at the last year or those final months, consider the time period immediately before. Figure out how long the last third of your career will last. For some, it will be five years; for others, a bit longer. This time should be spent building your path away from campus. Call a professional to help you make financial decisions, and review your progress every year. Pick two or three areas where you'll spend your retirement time, like making furniture or building a local nonprofit, and start learning some of the skills you'll need now. Seek out new social networks so you'll have plenty of friends to turn to later.

At the same time, you should set the path the school will continue to take after you've stepped into your new life. Find ways to pass on the capital built up by your years of experience. Mentor your assistant principal and any teacher who's expressed an interest in an administrative career track. Delegate the tasks principals need to perform to your mentees. Every week, write a few paragraphs about how you tackled a unique or a common problem that arose. Keep these briefs in a file or a notebook. By the time you're ready to leave, you'll be able to hand off a handbook stuffed with helpful advice.

These small steps, when performed over the last third of your career, will create a wealth of knowledge within your school. You'll also find that your mentees will become your greatest advocates. They might even turn into advisors you can call on when you need a sounding board. The entire time, you'll be building skills in several individuals who stand ready to step up. The collection of brief write-ups will be valuable touchstones for them. Or, if an entirely new person takes the helm, they'll have a source that reveals the school's history. You'll sail into retirement knowing that you've helped others carry into the future.

TELL WHY

Telling why means that you don't just give orders . . . you explain why things need to be done a certain way.

Telling why helps people understand the reasons certain things have to be done certain ways. When presented with rules, many people might go along with them but still question the wisdom behind the rules. When you explain why, you give everyone the opportunity to buy into the wisdom. When they take that wisdom on as their own, they work harder to make things happen the way your school needs them to happen.

Telling why becomes particularly important with unpopular decisions. Parents might not understand why certain extracurricular activities are no longer offered. They're so used to hearing about budget cuts that explaining this might not be enough. But if you tell them that budget cuts have resulted in an inability to staff the activities in a way that creates a safe and secure atmosphere, they see the wisdom of your decision and are more supportive.

Tell why whenever something changes, something starts, or something ends. Always provide the primary reason why something happens. Whenever possible, discuss one or two important secondary reasons. Don't share more than three to avoid confusion. By providing two or three reasons why, you broadcast the detail with which your decision was made. You assure everyone that the nuances have been considered and that the best decision was made using the best available information.

MAKE A STATEMENT

Make a statement to communicate more effectively across all the groups in your school.

Making a statement ensures that people will listen now and in the future. Whenever you make a statement, you're demonstrating that the information is important enough to treat in a special way. Statements are far more memorable than the usual flow of information, so they stand out from the inundation of news and tidbits that cross everyone's devices.

Make a statement whenever you need buy-in on a project or idea. If your school scores poorly in reading comprehension, bring in the books you read over the summer and stack them on a pedestal in front of the library. Challenge students to stack the books they read during the academic year on a table nearby and offer a prize for the stack with the most books. Ask teachers to display several age-appropriate titles that were important to them as kids in their classrooms. Encourage parents to send in quotes from titles that moved them when they were young. Make the statement that reading is important for more than just school to enhance engagement at every level.

Tailor your statement to the specific group. The statements you make to students should be fun, outrageous, and captivating. The statements you make to teachers and staff can be fun; they can also be thoughtful in ways that connect you on a more personal basis to the individuals with whom you work. Statements to parents might be moving, share your journey as an academic "parent" to their children, or funny. You know your people best. Make the type of statement that will reach them!

BE THE CCO: THE CHIEF CREATIVE OFFICER

Being the chief creative officer (CCO) means you foster an environment in which creative ideas and risk-taking is supported.

Being the CCO allows you and your people to explore possibilities and follow their curiosity to new places and into new ideas. Believe in their ability to generate positive outcomes even if you can't follow every idea right away. Encouraging new ideas pushes your students, their success, and your school to new heights!

Be the CCO by supporting even ideas that don't fit the mold. Sometimes the biggest and brightest innovations aren't feasible under current conditions. Ebooks were available for years before a single company sank enough money and effort into creating a relatively inexpensive reader. Electric cars have been around for a while, but there simply aren't enough charging stations . . . yet. When an idea fits your school but isn't feasible in the moment, don't allow it to die. Nurture it until the time is right to implement that one truly great idea!

Be the CCO using the best-of-your people skills. Engage with people at every level. Ask them about the challenges and opportunities they see. Listen to what they're thinking. Apply your wisdom and experience to find the ideas that are right for your school. Decide which ones to champion and then support them until they become real. As the CCO, you'll allow everyone the freedom to build a new school atop the foundation you've worked so hard to create.

PERSONAL PLAYLIST

Work up a personal playlist of music, sonic hues, or natural sounds to improve your mental health and create a portable distraction-free zone.

A personal playlist is a portable way to calm down, focus, and maintain a positive outlook no matter where you work. Noises in the environment distract and disturb us not necessarily because they're loud or unpleasant, but because the sound causes a sudden change in what we're hearing. Our brains pick up the change and, to protect us, attempts to analyze the source and whether it's a threat. This explains why a dripping faucet can be as nerve-wracking as the sudden roar of a coffee grinder.

When you setup a personal playlist of music or natural sounds, you block the unexpected intrusions with songs you know and love. You also reap the benefits associated with listening to music or the sounds of nature, which include reducing stress, elevating mood, and enhancing blood flow. Since music also tends to engage more regions of the brain than other activities, listening to your playlist can suppress disruptive random thoughts that might arise when your brain is engaged only with the work.

When you delve into sonic hues, your personal playlist can include the well-known white noise or be composed from pink or brown noise. White noise has long been recognized as beneficial for blocking other sounds because it presents tones from all audible frequencies at an equal level. Think of the static between radio stations, and you'll get an idea of what you'll hear. Pink noise also contains all audible frequencies, but presents the higher frequencies at a reduced volume. The sound of steady rain or wind is fairly close to pink noise. Brown noise goes a step further and dials down the higher frequencies even more. Brown noise resembles a roaring wind or the current of a strong river.

Fortunately, it's easy to set up a personal playlist with natural sounds or sonic hues. Plenty of ambient sound apps are available for smartphones and laptops. Many of the apps focus on one area, providing a variety of natural sounds or a variety of sonic hues. Be aware that the apps with looped sounds will start to feel repetitive after a while. You can get more mileage out of your app by switching between sounds now and then. You can also pick an app that uses naturally recorded sounds from cities or forests. Whatever you decide to use, your playlist will calm your mind and help you stay focused.

ADAPT, DON'T REACT

Adapt, don't react provides you with the flexibility to respond to situations as they arise . . . and prevents you from reacting in ways that might be fast but will turn out to be detrimental.

Adapt, don't react has two major benefits. First, it develops a flexible mind-set that allows you to manage a situation until it can be fully and properly addressed. Second, knowing that you can adapt prevents you from knee-jerk reactions that might exacerbate negative effects.

Adapt, don't react works exceptionally well in the educational environment. Every time you call in a substitute to cover for a sick teacher, you're adapting to a minor crisis. Whenever you sit down to talk with a student about misbehavior, you maintain a flexible attitude and gather the information you need to address the behavior. Adapt to every issue as it arises and you'll arrive at a measured, appropriate solution.

In many cases, adapt, don't react is built into your operational procedures. For issues that require you to adapt in the moment, follow three easy steps. First, step back from the situation on an emotional level. Second, gather as much information as you can. Finally, decide on the appropriate response. Many new situations can be handled by applying policies that already exist. When you need to address something totally new, blend elements of existing policies to tailor the solution to the situation.

TAKE IT PERSONALLY

Taking it personally connects you with the people whose needs, desires, and goals are fulfilled through your school.

Taking it personally recognizes that you, your staff, the students, and their parents all have a personal stake in your school. For very different reasons, each group is driven to ensure the success of individuals as well as the school's overall performance. When you take your job personally, you honor the goals of every person walking the halls.

Taking it personally is all about attitude. When you care enough to interact with students, they feel that your support is real and significant. When you listen to your teachers, they understand that your goals and theirs align. When you provide venues in which parents can interact with you and your staff, they recognize that the entire school is working hard for their children's futures. Taking your job personally is one of the best things you can do for yourself and for others!

Take it personally every day. Make time for individuals who need to bring up issues or who just want to chat about what's working well. Look people in the eye and turn fully toward them to convey your attention. Congratulate high achievers as well as those who are making an effort to grow. Encourage troubled individuals with supportive words. Consistent efforts on your part result in consistent efforts from everyone else. Take it personally . . . because they already do.

PUT YOURSELF IN TIME-OUT

Put yourself in time-out so you can step back, take a breath, and consider what's really going on.

Putting yourself in time-out gives you perspective on situations that might be confounding or irritating. It reduces your stress load . . . always a plus for principals! Your calm demeanor in turn calms other people down. When you integrate time-outs throughout the day, your mind is refreshed and your productivity and efficiency are enhanced.

Put yourself in time-out anytime you feel stressed. Even if you know what to do, take a time-out and encourage others to do the same. By sitting or standing quietly with you for a moment, most individuals will gain at least some control of their emotions and anxieties. Then, when you reengage in the discussion, they will be better able to hear the solution. They will walk away trusting your advice and will be far less likely to sink beneath the same problem in the future.

In critical circumstances, put yourself in time-out with this simple move. Hold up one hand and break eye contact with the individual. Look down or close your eyes for a moment. Let them see you take a deep breath; you'll be surprised how often people will mimic you and take their own deep breath. Stand for 10 seconds or so in this silent time-out. Then meet the individual's gaze. Now you can ask for more information, offer sympathy, or work toward a solution together!

MODEL BEHAVIOR

Principals who model behaviors they want to see in their schools become trusted leaders for everyone involved with the campus.

Modeling behaviors might seem like a given when it comes to heading up a school, but being able to convey expectations through actions isn't a trait that comes naturally to everyone. What your body language or word choices convey, for example, might not be on your radar. But they should be, along with a number of other simple steps that will model the kinds of behaviors you want to see on your campus.

First and foremost, be consistent. If you implement a policy of transparency, maintain that policy every time it's called for. During those times when you need to preserve individual privacy or have other reasons to hold information close, be transparent about the reasons for keeping certain details out of the public realm.

Next, provide clarity in your communications. When you simply model behaviors, others might not pick up on your intent. Broadcast your intention by pointing out similar behaviors among your staff and students. At times, you can even point out this behavior in yourself. You might, for example, ask for input about how the school is managing teachers' needs. Phrase your request using specific terms such as "I'm asking you to evaluate me." This will help people who might be distracted or less socially well versed understand that you expect others to be equally open to feedback.

Take care with your language. Use words and phrases the group is familiar with to call attention to the behavior you're modeling. When you speak to students, select accessible words and simple phrasing to call out how you support your peers. With parents, use words associated with achievement and advancement to advocate for calm leadership at home. For your people, drop the academic buzzwords. Talk to them like peers to convey your very real desire to support them fully, and to see them supporting each other. The more directly you tie the message to the model, the more your school will follow your lead.

TRUST YOURSELF

Trusting yourself develops your confidence in your abilities while it develops trust in those you lead.

Trusting yourself is a core command for principals. When you trust your own abilities, you convey the confidence others need to trust your leadership. Trust allows you to move ahead without unjustified doubts that might tangle your judgment. Trusting yourself conveys that you are trustworthy, and generates a secure, stable atmosphere.

Trust yourself because without you, the school sinks. Even though different classrooms and departments have their own leaders, the school as an organization needs one person in command. You are the person everyone turns to in good times and bad. You are the individual that parents, students, and the community rely on for a bright future. You have been selected for this role because you have the experience, dedication, and knowledge to lead the school forward. Trusting yourself provides you with the same stability and confidence you offer everyone in your community.

Trust yourself every day. When things are going well, consider how easy it is to trust your judgments and decisions. Recognize how smoothly things operate because you have guided the many small steps that generate progress. When things get rough, you can trust yourself because you have consciously recognized how trusting in yourself has benefited the school in the past! Trust is truly the defining core of every successful principal.

DO YOUR "HOMEWORK"

Doing your homework creates a community that centers on your school.

Doing your homework weaves all the different components—teachers, students, parents, and others—into a tapestry that spreads far beyond campus. When individuals are more aware of the school, they are more likely to pitch in, promote, and participate.

Doing your homework allows schools to reach beyond their current level. Schools that are suffering from budget cuts, lack of parental participation, and other common issues can bolster their resources by drawing from the broader community. Student bodies that are not performing well will achieve more when they recognize that their efforts impact their families and friends. When principals do their homework, teachers and staff feel like they are an intrinsic part of the broader community. They feel supported!

Do your homework with the many resources and organizations that already exist. Send monthly announcements to local and regional papers for school plays, sports events, and other activities. Reach out to bloggers who write about education and parenting, and connect them with your students and teachers. Invite local photographers, painters, and authors in for brief tours so that they can take inspiration from the campus environment . . . then share the results with the larger community.

SCHEDULE SELF-CARE

Take a big step for your mental, emotional, and physical well-being by scheduling self-care the same way you schedule tasks.

Dedicated educators, especially those in leadership roles, too often place themselves at the bottom of their to-do list. In addition to negatively impacting their physical health, pushing their own needs away leaves them with less energy for the work they love and the people they help. Rather than waiting for a free hour (or minutes) to magically appear, schedule self-care into your daily, weekly, and monthly routines.

Before you wonder how you'll ever fit self-care into your day, know that you don't need to block out large chunks of time. A quick walk, five minutes of listening to music, or fifteen minutes spent reading a short story or one chapter from a novel will signal your body to relax. Engaging actively with something other than work will turn your mind toward pleasure. If you don't want to fit this into your work routine, try waking up earlier. Spend the first fifteen minutes of your day breathing deeply, stretching, or walking through your neighborhood. Mirror those minutes with another block of time doing the same activity before you go to sleep. Accessing the relaxed mode brought about by this quick break will deliver a truly restful night.

Every week, dedicate an additional half hour to scheduled self-care. Because you have a bit more time in your weekly block, you can walk further or stop at a park on the way home. Instead of stretching in your bedroom, you might power walk or jog a mile, clean up your flowerbed, or engage in other hobbies. Flip through a family scrapbook or write a letter (yes, by hand, to keep you away from your computer) to a friend. What you do during this time isn't as important as picking an activity that is unconnected to your work.

Once a month, carve out two hours on your schedule of self-care. Meet a friend for coffee or invite your spouse on a hike. Take your kids for a drive and stop for ice cream or at a pick-your-own farm. Attend a yoga or weightlifting class to guide your daily self-care exercise sessions. Or simply sit on the porch with the local paper and a cup of coffee. Whether you take this as two one-hour blocks or a single two-hour segment, you'll end up with more to offer others because you've given so much to yourself.

RESPECT YOURSELF

Respect yourself means that you extend the same compassion to your own efforts as you do to others.

Respect yourself to get the most out of your career and to give the most to your school. Offer yourself the same compassion and forgiveness you offer others when you make a mistake. Respect your acumen and abilities to build the confidence to tackle any situation, no matter how tough.

Respect yourself in good times and bad. We've all encountered that one parent who harps on every little thing that goes wrong. We also work in a field where accomplishments are rarely recognized because the highest expectations are built into our careers and our personalities. Respect yourself by recognizing—not just once in a while but regularly—the enormity of the job you've undertaken. Respect the extraordinary accomplishments you've already achieved!

Respect yourself daily using a pocket-sized journal. At the end of every day, record one thing you're proud to have accomplished that day.

It might be something small, like the moment when you connected with a troubled student. It could be something big like landing that funding grant. When you've filled up the journal, label the spine with the dates and then place it somewhere visible. Every day you can look at the shelf of accomplishments and get a boost!

ADD ALLIES

Adding allies builds a group of individuals who will support you and your vision for the school.

Adding allies builds a supportive network. Someone who listens without judgment, who understands where you're coming from and where you're going can help put your thoughts in order and relieve stress. These people can also provide new ideas. Having them around is powerful in and of itself!

Adding allies proved extremely valuable for Principal Carol Birks of Warren Harding High in Bridgeport, Connecticut. A week before school opened, she held a community forum to share her vision for the upcoming year. Because of her call for help, community involvement increased a whopping 90 percent. What principal wouldn't like to see that kind of improvement!

When you add allies, remember that these individuals don't have to be experts. They might not even be on campus; small businesses, corporate representatives, homeschoolers, and others can offer different kinds of support. Most of your allies, though, will come from the school community. Engage parents, teachers, administrative staff, and even students. When people from a variety of groups help out, you're much more likely to bring your vision to life.

SPECIALIZED ASSISTANCE

Because principals have to tackle so many areas, call for specialized assistance when a specific skillset is required to address a challenge.

Every campus has a host of needs that don't fall under the academic rubric. These include everything from safety concerns and crisis response to the ever-evolving psychosocial landscape. When you're facing a challenge in an area that falls even a little outside the academic realm, reach for specialized assistance from individuals who have experience in that arena.

As an example, safety and security are at the top of many school lists. Fortunately, principals have a host of ways to receive specialized assistance, and many of those options are free. Connect with your local police department, fire rescue team, and first responders when you're reviewing campus safety plans. Have someone tour your facilities to pinpoint areas where improvements can be made. Often, these same people can explain how to handle each issue. If they don't, they might be able to pass you on to a different agency or organization that can help.

Don't hesitate to reach out to individuals and businesses that would normally charge for their services. Connect with a large event planner in your area and have them review your facilities and event safety plans. In exchange, offer them a write-up in the newsletter you send out to the community about the service they provided. They'll gain attention from a new group of potential customers as well as something called "corporate goodwill." Large companies spend more money advertising the good deeds they perform than they ever funneled into the deed itself. Corporate goodwill is worth that much.

Recognize, too, that you can ask for specialized assistance in areas that will provide intangible benefits. Set up a mental health fair, and give organizations in your area tables in the gym. Be sure to include nonprofits, individual practitioners, and government agencies. Invite parents, teachers, and students to browse the booths. Let the sports team sell sodas and power bars to fund their teams, and provide a coloring booth where kids can paint or draw to make the day a go-to event. By offering avenues to areas outside of academic opportunities, you'll help your community live full and happy lives.

SUMMER SESSIONS

Summer sessions allow you to engage with the school community during a period when you have the time to really focus on individuals.

The uniqueness of summer sessions catches people's attention . . . and proves your dedication in a real and meaningful way. Taking time to meet with individuals when school isn't in session provides a more relaxed way to connect. When people are comfortable, they're able to think more clearly and provide feedback that's detailed and honest.

Summer sessions are about listening. Bill Carozza, Principal of Harold Martin Elementary in Hopkinton, New Hampshire, uses summer sessions to speak with paraprofessionals, administrative staff, kitchen workers, and custodians. He asks for input on what's working well and ways things could be improved. A review of the information helps direct the goals he sets for the coming year.

Implement summer sessions by connecting with individuals through e-mail lists. Send out an announcement of your intent at the end of the year. Then set up interviews with individuals who respond first. Contact individuals who didn't reply to tell them their input is valuable. This is especially important if you find that you have a lot of input from one demographic but little from another. When people hear about those specific needs, they'll be much more likely to participate. As you repeat your summer sessions, people will begin to expect them and response rates will rise.

BODY CHECK

To reduce longstanding stress and head off the impact of new stressors, perform a body check to monitor your natural survival instincts.

Stress, anxiety, and frustration all trigger powerful physical responses. The human body responds to the world with a complex interaction of hormonal signals, neural messages, and activity in the muscles and organs. Whenever you feel anxious or upset, the body ramps up the different systems to make sure you survive whatever threat you're facing. While these responses can save us from danger, in our modern world, they tend to be triggered by things that aren't truly dangerous. The body doesn't know that a full-on brawl isn't required, so we end up suffering chronic stress or acute stress.

Perform a body check by sitting or lying down in a peaceful environment. Take a few deep breaths and focus your attention in the middle of your head just behind your eyes. Once you feel "present" in that space, move your focus down your neck and spine. Follow each arm down to the fingers. Then move your attention along each leg to the toes. As your attention shifts, note any aches, pains, or feelings of discomfort in any limb or your head or torso. Once you've paid attention to your entire body, recall the places that have pain or discomfort. Return your attention to those places and, using your imagination, simply "look" at each area for a minute or two.

Once you've paid attention to each uncomfortable area, take a deep breath and stand up. Move the achy joint or gently rub the painful area. The most common physical impacts of stress are headaches, sour stomachs or nausea, tightness in the chest, tight and tired muscles (particularly in the neck), low back pain, and elevated heart rates or blood pressure. If you find that the body check isn't soothing the symptoms, consider learning tai chi or getting a massage. Tai chi can be particularly helpful because it focuses on physical balance while toning muscles and moving all the body's joints.

Of course, you'll also want to continue your usual self-care habits. If you haven't set up a schedule for self-care yet, performing a body check will prove how much you need to regularly nurture and support your physical and mental well-being. Those who already have a solid self-care routine might consider adding more elements to the existing schedule. Or you might take time to laugh. Watching a funny movie, swapping jokes with your kids, and finding touches of humor as you go about your day are some of the most powerful medicines you can take.

CULTIVATE COURAGE

Cultivate courage in yourself. Being a principal is a tough job! You're not always going to be popular, and things aren't always going to be easy. With courage, you can be the champion your school needs.

Cultivating courage starts with you and spreads outward. When others see how you persevere, they are inspired to do the same. Courage gives you the confidence to undertake even the most challenging tasks. Courage allows you to stand tall when facing issues that might overwhelm others. As a principal, you must lead with courage.

Cultivating courage is one of the most important things you can do for your students and your community. Principals are involved in the daily lives and ongoing education of nearly 50 million children in the United States. As such, they are one of the biggest influences on the present and future of our citizens and our country. Leaders need courage to lead properly and nowhere is that more evident than at the helm of our schools.

Cultivate courage by knowing that you can do what you set out to do. As much as possible, make yourself immune to the naysayers whose agendas are served by attacking you, your teachers, and your school. Recognize that your experience, when combined with the experience of your staff, equals decades or even centuries of wisdom. Know that you are surrounded by individuals whose hearts overflow with best intentions. Take strength from these resources and your courage will become your armor!

Final Words
Always a Principal

Always a principal reminds you that once you've stepped into this role, you'll be a principal for the rest of your life!

You are always a principal on a nonstop cycle that has no end. In the middle of the night, you will still be the principal when there is an emergency at the school. If you ever move into a higher position, you will still be called on to support principals as a fellow former principal. And even after you retire, you will still be viewed by the community as a leader!

Always a principal is really based on one key element present in all great principals: they enter this job field because they want every child to receive the very best education possible. Because this type of job shifts frequently—sometimes every day—with every new opportunity and in the light of new studies, a principal's job is never done. They know that going in . . . and because they never plan to be finished, they will always be a principal!

By reading this book, you have already proven that you will always be a principal. Truly nothing I can suggest or recommend is going to change who you already are. So instead, I'll offer my heartfelt thanks from one principal to another. *Thank you for being who you are!*

About the Author

Barbara D. Culp, M.A.Ed., Ed.D. has dedicated forty-three years of her life to education as a teacher, principal, and clinical supervisor. She founded a tutorial service for public, private, charter, and parochial schools, through which she offers workshops and training programs on classroom management and differentiated instruction. Recently, she began offering online coaching sessions to parents who wish to help their students achieve the highest level of academic success. Dr. Culp has been featured in *Voyage ATL* and *Shoutout Atlanta.* In 2020, *The Art of Appraisal* took gold in the Nonfiction Authors Association competition.

www.ingramcontent.com/pod-product-compliance
Lightning Source LLC
Chambersburg PA
CBHW032301150426
43195CB00008BA/530